Learning About
WINTER
with Children's Literature

Learning About
WINTER
with Children's Literature

Cross-curricular units based on the works of Frank Asch, Ezra Jack Keats, Tomie de Paola, and more

Margaret A. Bryant, Marjorie Keiper, and Anne Petit

Zephyr Press

Chicago

Cover design: Monica Baziuk

© 2006 by Margaret A. Bryant, Marjorie Keiper, and Anne Petit
All rights reserved
Published by Zephyr Press
An imprint of Chicago Review Press, Incorporated
814 North Franklin Street
Chicago, Illinois 60610
ISBN-10: 1-56976-205-8
ISBN-13: 978-1-56976-205-9
Printed in the United States of America

DEDICATION

To Keith, Glenn, and Jim—
without your support this book could not have been written
and
to the First Graders of Old Trail School
—past, present, and future—
you were our inspiration

CONTENTS

INTRODUCTION

About the Program

The early primary classroom presents many challenges to the teacher who must provide an environment that nurtures strengths, addresses needs, develops strong academic skills, and encourages a positive self-concept. Students may be knowledgeable about many things but may lack some basic experiences that are necessary for success in an academic setting. A whole language approach can build a foundation that gives all students an opportunity to succeed.

We define whole language as a holistic approach to the teaching of reading and writing. A whole language approach employs seeing, hearing, reading, and writing words to develop the competencies children need to become fluent, independent readers and writers. Phonetic skills, the foundation of a comprehensive literacy program, are presented during the daily poetry session.

Trade books offer the opportunity to learn to read through stories that are interesting, support in-depth and varied questioning, and encourage a love of literature in young children. These books establish a common ground that allows students who have had limited experience with books to interact with more privileged peers. The content also provides a basis for higher-level questioning and enrichment activities that will challenge more capable students.

We are aware of the wide range of abilities found in most early primary classrooms. At the age some children are independent learners while others are still struggling to grasp basic skills and need many opportunities for reinforcement. It takes a magician to create a warm, nurturing environment in which children with such differing needs will be successful. This book offers ideas for the child who is an emerging reader as well as for those children who are reading far above their grade level. The common books and themes of this program give all students the opportunity to interact successfully while being challenged at the appropriate instructional level. Because children of varying abilities use the same material, although in different ways, emerging readers do not feel that they are in a different reading group.

The whole language approach encourages children to view writing as positively as they view reading. Inability to spell a word does not prevent a child from using it. The child simply writes the sounds he or she hears or, early on, the first letter, and draws a line for the remainder of the word. Confidence, competency, and fluency develop rapidly in this accepting atmosphere.

Thematic units incorporate other subjects into the reading program. As teachers are being asked to include more and more in the curriculum, this method of organization allows maximum use of the school day. The broad range of available trade books makes it easy to meet science or social studies objectives while children are receiving reading instruction.

A limited budget may be a factor in establishing a program that relies on trade books. Although it is ideal to have many copies of the books when implementing this program, other options exist. One rather time-consuming possibility is to get many copies from school and community libraries. If only one copy is available, you can read the story to the class, have the children choose eighteen to twenty words from that story for instructional purposes, and then have children rewrite the story in their own words. You can then copy this story on chart paper, the chalkboard, or individual sheets for students to use during instructional reading time.

One advantage of the latter method is that the children identify with the story and have a sense of ownership, which can be powerful tool for young readers because what they write they are also able to read. For example, if you are using *If You Give a Mouse a Cookie*, students may choose *refrigerator* as one of the focal words. Though this word is not typically considered a first-grade word, it has high interest value, and less exciting (but just as useful) words must be employed to create a sentence. Thus *refrigerator* becomes the tool to help children learn words such as *the* and *that*.

Structure of Plans

Lesson plans are keyed with the following symbols:

EL (emerging learners): Children who are working below grade level or need extra support

TL (typical learners): Students who are performing at grade level

AL (advanced learners): Children whose abilities require more challenging activities

Whole language is a successful method for teaching young children to read, write, and spell, but because it is less structured than a basal program, some teachers are reluctant to use it. This book offers a way to support all the skills necessary for creating a strong literacy foundation for young children. Although you can introduce skills in a variety of ways, we have made suggestions for presenting skills on a weekly basis. In this program, all basic skills are introduced, reinforced, and assessed.

We suggest group instruction for introducing a reading selection, but you will also have many opportunities for small-group and individual instruction. You will need to group children as their needs dictate for reteaching or remedial work. Typically, some students will understand and master skills the first time they are presented, whereas other children will need several sessions. You will have to determine what is best for the children in your classroom.

Poetry and Skills

Poems are an obvious vehicle for teaching rhyming words, but they are equally effective for learning vowels, blends, and contractions, as well as other skills necessary for a child to become a strong, independent reader. In the program described here, the skills lessons are presented to the whole class during shared reading of the daily poem.

We have selected poems to coordinate with the thematic units. In our program, children memorize one poem each month. During the first week of the month, you will introduce the poem, discuss it, and display it in a prominent place. You will give each child a copy to illustrate and place in an individual poetry notebook and another to take home to memorize. When a child recites the poem, place a sticker on that page in the notebook. You might also write the child's name on a seasonal cut-out and attach it to the displayed poem. In our classrooms we have cut-outs that coordinate with the monthly theme. There is no award given to the first child who recites the poem nor any particular notice to the child who is last. The public record is merely a reminder to those who have not learned the poem, and it offers the teacher a quick check on the progress of the class.

How to Get Started

Educators often assume that children who are reading independently do not need the same skills lessons as typical readers or those who read below grade level. This assumption is a grave error. Although some children may read early, they may not know important labels or have decoding strategies, which can cause them problems later on. A child may be able to read "isn't," for example, but might not understand contractions. These students need to build the same foundation as their classmates, although they may be able to do so at a quicker pace.

Grouping

Our philosophy is that the daily lessons should be presented in whole group sessions, but we also recognize that children learn at different rates and have different needs. We have therefore organized the lessons so that the objective is introduced to the class as a whole, but direct instruction is handled in smaller groups.

Children will be placed in various groups for various instructional purposes. For example, after you introduce a new book you might place the students into small groups that have a mix of ability levels. Children will read the story orally, which allows the more capable students to support the emerging readers. In another session, children who need extra help with a particular decoding skill will meet in a small group for reinforcement. Although children will recognize the more fluent readers, when they are grouped for purposes other than ability, no one feels like a "crow" instead of a "bluebird." The sensitive teacher keeps groups fluid so children are comfortable with and have opportunities to interact with all their classmates.

Author of the Month

Each month an author is featured and several of his or her books are included in the reading plans. The students learn about the author's childhood, other careers he or she pursued, the author's struggle for perfection, and some of the obstacles that had to be overcome before the author gained recognition for his or her work. This material will help young readers gain an understanding of the person who wrote, and in many cases illustrated, the books.

Other children enjoy writing to authors, many of whom are sensitive to their young audiences and will respond to fan letters. Letters from authors should be kept in a scrapbook for the class, parents, and other interested parties to read. At the end of the year each letter should become the property of the child who received the letter. You can find addresses for authors at the reference desk of your local library or through the publisher.

Thematic Structure

This program employs a thematic approach that incorporates other subject areas into the reading program. Each month there is an academic focus around which the language arts block is organized.

Using Music

Music is an important part of all curriculum plans. Children are naturally expressive and should be encouraged to explore this expressiveness through musical experiences. The elements of rhythm, form, melody, and harmony contribute to the emotional quality of music. We intend the selections in this program to enhance children's appreciation for music. It will help young children appreciate and interpret musical messages if they have a basic understanding of the language of music. You can adapt the open-ended activities that follow for use with any musical selection chosen for the primary classroom.

Comparisons

To develop an awareness of the different means of expression used in music, select two different pieces, such as lullaby and a march. Play a recording of the lullaby and ask the children to verbalize how the music makes them feel. Play the march and ask them the same question. Encourage children to compare and contrast the two pieces. Your students could also move rhythmically to the music to feel how two different dances require the same or different body movements.

Scribble drawings

You can encourage students to express themselves to music through scribble drawings and tone paintings. For scribble drawings, ask students to make uninterrupted scribble designs with crayons on paper while listening to a musical selection. Later they can attempt to create from their scribbles forms that the music suggested.

Tone paintings

After listening to one (or more) pieces, children might paint their own interpretations while listening to the music.

Journals

Tempo and dynamics set many different moods. Help children learn to identify the various musical instruments and verbalize the feelings the instruments create after listening to a specific piece. Students could keep musical journals to record their thoughts on selections they have listened to and enjoyed. They might include musical illustrations in their journals.

Symbols and vocabulary

To help children understand the symbols and terms used to represent expression in music, cut tag board into strips—or use commercially prepared sentence strips—and on each strip write one of the following symbols or terms:

<	crescendo	gradually louder
>	decrescendo	gradually softer
f	forte	loud
ff	fortissimo	very loud
mf	mezzo forte	medium loud
mp	mezzo piano	medium soft
p	piano	soft
pp	pianissimo	very soft
	allegro	fast
	andante	slow
	moderato	moderately

Use the cards to make a game of matching terms and symbols. Or you might try passing out the cards to the children and asking questions such as, *If you have a card that means to play or sing very loudly, hold up your card.* You can also use the cards while you are listening to various selections. Have children hold up an appropriate card to describe what they hear happening in the music. They might be surprised to see how quickly the cards change and how often each one is used throughout the selection.

Scope and Sequence

This section offers an overview of each month's objectives. Our goal has been to organize the material in a flexible manner that will allow teachers to incorporate it into their individual curricula. Activities for science, social studies, math, music, art, and French are included in the weekly lessons, but not all subjects are included in each unit. Although the only foreign language we have included is French, many materials in other languages are available and can be substituted in accordance with the mandates of individual curricula.

DECEMBER

Author: Frank Asch

English Skills
   Phonetic skills
      Vowel digraphs
      Vowel with r
   Structural analysis
      Root words
Science Skills
   Seasons
      Animals in winter
         Bears
            Migration and hibernation

Social Studies Skills
   Holiday customs in
      Israel
      France
      Italy
      Mexico
      Germany
      England
      Russia
      United States
Music Skills
   The Nutcracker

JANUARY

Author: Frank Asch

English Skills
Phonetic Skills
  Consonant blends
    Beginning
    End
  Structural Analysis
    Synonyms
    Homonyms
    Antonyms
    Plural and possessive nouns
    Apostrophe
  Comprehension
    Comparing
    Contrasting
    Book reports

Science Skills
Birds
  Characteristics
  Identification and parts
  Adaptation for winter
Winter
  Signs of
  Adaptation of animals

Math Skills
Calendar
New year
Graphing of weather
Counting by 2

Social Studies Skills
Compare weather, seasons of
  two hemispheres

FEBRUARY

Author: Rita Gellman

English Skills
Phonetic skills
  Vowel diphthongs
  Endings -er, -est
Structural analysis
  Pronouns
  Verb tense
  Alphabetizing to second letter
Comprehension
  Categorizing
  Main idea
  Topic sentences
  Supporting facts

Science Skills
Human body
  Bones
  Lungs and breathing
  Heart and blood
  Brain and nerves
  Stomach and Digestion
  Skin
Health
  Nutrition
    Food groups

Social Studies Skills
History of pasta
Abraham Lincoln
George Washington

Math Skills
Calendar
Patterning
Categories

1
DECEMBER

Theme: Holiday Customs around the World

Author of the month: Frank Asch

This chapter uses holiday customs of various countries to develop an awareness of cultural differences and continues to help children master the social studies objectives introduced in the previous chapter. Because most schools have a two-week vacation at this time of the year, the work is organized into a time line that covers three weeks but may be adjusted as needed.

The social studies activities, at the end of the chapter, are not arranged by the week but as a whole to simplify planning and implementation of the lessons.

Week 1: Overview

Instructional Books

Happy Birthday Moon by Frank Asch
Moongame by Frank Asch

Related Titles

Corduroy by Don Freeman (to be read aloud)
Bears: A First Discovery Book by Gallimard Jeunesse and Laura Bour (to be read aloud)
Sierra Club Wildlife Library: Bears by Ian Stirling (to be read aloud)
Polar Express by Chris Van Allsburg (to be read aloud)

Poems

"Grizzly Bear" by Mary Austin
"December" by Maurice Sendak
"Grandpa Bear's Lullaby" by Jane Yolan

Music

"The Teddy Bear's Picnic"
The Nutcracker by Tchaikovsky

Objectives

1. **Structural analysis**
   Review the concept of root words.
   Review skills previously introduced and have them assessed.

2. **Comprehension**
   Vocabulary

3. **Social Studies**
   Compare and contrast holiday customs of different cultures.
   Develop an appreciation for the influence of these cultures on present customs.

Materials

Word cards in the shape of the moon and the hat worn by Bear

12-by-18-inch drawing paper

3-by-11-inch strips of construction paper

Brown construction paper

Poetry and Skills Session

DAY 1

"December"

Step 1: Read the poem together. Children will now be familiar with the form, and most will be able to read it with success.

Step 2: Identify rhyming words. Ask the students to offer some other rhymes for the poem. Examples: "Hanukkah tree with candle lights . . . " "Football tree with helmets and pads . . . " Encourage and accept all responses. This activity can be continued as a writing project.

Step 3: Distribute copies of the poem for your students to illustrate and include in their poetry notebooks.

DAY 2

"Grandpa Bear's Lullaby"

Step 1: Read the poem several times with the group. Discuss the meaning.

Step 2: Ask children to identify the root words. Mark them with an erasable pen if the poem is laminated.

Step 3: List the endings that have been added to the root words. Distribute copies of the poem for your students to illustrate and include in their poetry notebooks.

DAY 3

"Grandpa Bear's Lullaby"

Step 1: Read several times for rhythm and pleasure. Ask children to alternate reading the verses.

Step 2: Review the root words. Children who have trouble with root words should be grouped for individualized instruction.

Step 3: Make a list of words that have been changed through the use of endings.

DAY 4

"Grizzly Bear"

Step 1: Read this several times so the children can enjoy the humor in it.

Step 2: Ask the children to suggest other questions you might ask a grizzly bear.

Step 3: This poem provides an excellent opportunity for creative writing. Even a "silly" response may trigger an idea in another child. Write some variations of the poem on chart paper or the chalk board.

Step 4: Distribute copies of the poem for your students to illustrate and include in their poetry notebooks.

DAY 5

Children can choose the poetry they wish to read.

Reading Instruction

DAY 1

Biographical sketch of Frank Asch

Frank Asch was born on August 6, 1946, in Sommerville, New Jersey. As a young boy, he loved to play in the woods near his country home. He was happier there than he was in school. In school he sat either by the window so he could look out or in the back of the room, where the teacher would probably not call on him. The success he remembers in first grade was drawing an apple tree; the teacher heaped great praise upon him for the picture. He got no more recognition for his artistic accomplishments until high school, when he walked into the art room and saw an entire board labeled, "Frank Asch—One-Man Show."

Since leaving school, Mr. Asch has lived in New York, California, and India. He has been a library storyteller, done puppetry and children's theater, and taught in a Montessori preschool. He still performs story-theater productions for children, for which he writes the material and his wife supplies the music. Their company is called "Bellybuttons" (de Montreville & Crawford 1978).

Happy Birthday Moon

Shared Reading

Step 1: Introduce the *Happy Birthday Moon* big book. Discuss the fact that Mr. Asch both wrote and illustrated the book.

Step 2: Note the dedication. Many of his books are dedicated to "Devin." As the books are read, the children may notice this and begin to ask questions about it. This interest can be a springboard for writing letters to the author.

Step 3: Read the book together. Allow time for the children to enjoy the humor in the story and make comments about the activities of Bear.

Step 4: Discuss Mr. Asch's stylized illustrations. The simplicity of the pictures reflects the childlike qualities of Bear. He believes that it is possible to talk to the moon if you just get high enough. He has no doubt that he can build a rocket that will take him to the moon to see how it tastes. Bear's innocence is reflected in the simple forms, clear lines, and limited use of colors in the illustrations. The drawings lack detail and are simple almost to the point of being clichés.

Small Group Instruction

Step 1: Mix abilities for guided reading of student copies.

Step 2: Ask questions that can be answered by finding sentences on the page. Let various children read the sentences aloud. Offer assistance as needed.

Step 3: Make note of difficult vocabulary. Select fifteen to twenty words for focus. Write these on cards cut in the shape of a moon and a top hat.

DAY 2

Happy Birthday Moon

Shared Reading

Step 1: Reread the big book together. Have small groups take different parts of the story. One child can be the narrator, some can be Bear, others can read the moon's part. The latter lends itself to dramatization as the volume changes like an echo. Encourage the children to have fun with it.

Step 2: Identify rhyming words.

Small Group Instruction

EL: Work with the vocabulary words. Have each child choose a word and use it in a sentence. Then select more difficult words and read them. Have the children find a word on a page and then read aloud the sentence in which it appears.

TL:

Step 1: Discuss Bear's motives in the story.

Step 2: List adjectives that describe Bear. Use various vocabulary words in sentences to describe him.

Step 3: Ask which part of the story could be true. Which part is purely fiction? Let individuals choose a favorite page and read it to the group.

AL:

Step 1: Read the story silently for enjoyment.

Step 2: Encourage the group to discuss the appealing qualities of Bear.

Step 3: Ask which parts of the story are the most difficult to believe. Why? If the children were writing the story, what would they change?

Step 4: Have the children choose a present they would give Moon and write a story about it.

DAY 3

Moongame

Shared Reading

Step 1: Introduce the big book of *Moongame*. Ask for predictions about the story. Write these on a chart or chalkboard, and evaluate them after the story has been read.

Step 2: Read the book. Encourage discussion of similarities with *Happy Birthday Moon*. A Venn diagram is useful for this comparison.

Small Group Instruction

EL:

Step 1: If this group is ready for new material, follow the same procedure as with *Happy Birthday Moon*. If they need more time to master the vocabulary, don't introduce the new book.

Step 2: Find the words that are nouns, verbs, and adjectives. Read the words together. Arrange them in alphabetical order.

Step 3: Have the children read the story with a partner. (Take this opportunity to observe and evaluate comprehension and vocabulary development.)

TL: Read *Moongame*, using comprehension questions to guide the reading. Allow time for discussion of illustrations and comparison with *Happy Birthday Moon*.

AL: Read *Moongame* silently. Encourage discussion of the books and their similarities and differences with other Asch books. Have the students write literature reports comparing the two books.

DAY 4

Polar Express

Shared Reading

Step 1: Read *Polar Express* to the group. Allow time for the children to comment on the story and the illustrations. Encourage them to draw parallels between the dream-like quality of both the story and the pictures. Mr. Van Allsburg's use of color and line creates this quality in the illustrations.

Step 2: Compare these pictures to those of Mr. Asch. Discuss what the creators may be trying to say through the pictures. Broaden the discussion to include other authors with whom they are familiar.

Small Group Instruction

EL: Using the vocabulary, have the children compose a story about a bear and write it on chart paper or the chalkboard. Duplicate it for their use. Distribute large drawing paper and fold it in half (hamburger fold). Illustrate the story on one half, saving the other side to mount the story they have written.

Allow time for this group to read their story to the class or to a friend.

TL: Have the students read the book silently. Address any vocabulary that is troubling them. These words should be written unobtrusively on a slip of paper during the silent reading session. After the book has been read, put the words on the board and suggest means of decoding them. In this way, no child is embarrassed when asking for help. Usually they will see some words they knew that someone else did not.

AL:

- The literature reports done in the previous session are used as the basis of this discussion. Have the students share their reports with the group. Respond favorably to all, but help students appreciate the subtle differences that may have been observed.

- Ask again for adjectives that describe Bear. Extend the list that is being formed, encouraging the explanations of choices. The stage might be set for the children by stating, "I think Bear is very innocent." This will encourage them to ask for an explanation and model the kind of discussion desired.

DAY 5

Shared Reading

- Place both Asch big books side by side and discuss them. Which was the favorite? Why?

- Read both stories. Find vocabulary and phrases that are the same in both books.

- Discuss where Mr. Asch might get ideas for these stories. Could they come from a child? What would be some other ideas for stories?

Small Group Instruction

EL:

- This session should produce successful experiences for this group. Allow students to read the story written during the previous session. Make favorable comments about the story.

- Let them choose a page from one of the Bear books to read aloud, either alone or with a partner.

TL: Read the book as a play, with children taking the parts of the characters and the narrator and one providing sound effects. Do this several times so that all have the opportunity to participate equally.

AL:

Step 1: Make a sequence chain of one of the books. Distribute strips of paper, 3 by 11 inches. The children write sentences about what happened in the story on each of the strips. These are pasted together to form a sequence chain. The children can draw, cut out, and paste a brown bear to the first circle.

Step 2: Share the chains with the group, and then hang them in a window or other prominent place, commenting on those who have taken time to do an exceptional job.

Independent Activities

Materials

Books for writing activities

Writing and construction paper

Several empty boxes that have been gift wrapped so the top can be removed

Green construction paper cut in the shape of fir trees

Construction paper cut in shapes of bears and honey pots

Extension Activities

- Begin individual bear books based on information learned while reading the nonfiction titles. As each bear is studied, have the children draw a picture of that bear, write several sentences about it at the bottom of the picture, and place it in a folder until all have been presented. Combine the pages into a book, add a cover, and let the children name and decorate their book. (This is a good tool for the evaluation of comprehension, writing skills, and task completion.)

- *Happy Birthday Moon* offers several possibilities for literature extension. The idea of giving the moon a birthday present delights young children. Suggest that they think of one. It will be necessary to get this present to the moon, so they must devise a method of transporting it. Write a story describing the present and how it will be conveyed to the moon. Illustrate the story with a picture or, if time permits, allow the children to 'build' the illustration with construction paper. (This is a good use for the paper in the scrap box.)

- Make a holiday dictionary by presenting the children with blank books constructed from writing paper, stapled inside a construction paper cover. Using half-page sections, write a letter of the alphabet on each page. Throughout the month, add words under the appropriate letter. Small illustrations can follow each word.

Small Group and Center Activities

- Place the words from the Asch books in the bottom of a gift box. Put the box on a table so the children can play games with the words.

- Write math facts on small Christmas tree shapes. Cut the trees apart so that the problem and answer are on different parts of the tree. Place these in a basket or other attractive container for students to match.

- Cut out bear and honey pot shapes. Write a contraction on the bear and the words that make up the contraction on the honey pot. Place the shapes in a container and have the children match them.

- Cover three small boxes with gift paper. Label one "nouns," the second "verbs," and the third "adjectives." Write words on colored circles to represent decorations for a Christmas tree. On the back of each word, write N (noun), V (verb), or A (adjective). The children are to place the words in the correct box. One child in the group is the checker. After the words have been sorted, the checker turns each word over to see whether it is in the correct box.

Science

Objectives

Identify seven species of bears.
Understand the concept of hibernation.
Learn about the habits, diet, and behavior of bears.

Discuss the following characteristics of bears:

- Bears are mammals. They have fur, give birth to young, and nourish the young with milk from the mother's body.

- Bears are not true hibernators. They sleep during the winter but wake on warm days to look for food.

- Bears usually give birth to two cubs during the winter. Cubs are tiny but grow rapidly.

- There are eight species of bears. From smallest to largest they are as follows:

  Sun bear: the smallest of the bears, it is found in lowland forests of southeast Asia.
  Panda bear: it lives in a small area of China.
  Sloth bear: it lives in the jungles of Sri Lanka, Pakistan, and India.
  Asiatic black bear: this bear is found in southern and southeast Asia.
  American black bear: North America is home to this bear.
  Spectacled bear: this is the only bear found in South America.
  Brown bear: it lives throughout the world and includes the grizzly.
  Polar bear: it is found through the Arctic regions (Stirling 1992).

Math

Prepare a life-size graph of bears. Measure the length of a polar bear on a long piece of butcher paper. Mark the height of this bear. Have children draw pictures and record information about them.

As each bear is studied, add its height to the graph. Hang the completed graph on the wall of the room or in the hall. This gives children a concrete visual concept of the comparative sizes of bears.

Foreign Language

Introduce descriptive words related to bears: colors, sizes, temperament, and body parts.

Music

"The Teddy Bears' Picnic" provides opportunity for creative movement to accompany the study of bears. The idea of visualizing a group of bears having a picnic will encourage creative thoughts. What will the bears eat? What games will they play?

Play the musical score from *The Nutcracker* frequently during this month. It can be played as the children arrive in the morning, during silent reading time, during an independent work period, or as you deem appropriate. The objective is to become familiar with the music so that when the children see the video, they will be able to follow the story more easily.

Art

The music from *The Nutcracker* offers many opportunities to connect music with artistic expression. Play "Dance of the Sugar Plum Fairy" from *The Nutcracker*. Have the children draw a picture as suggested by the music. Use watercolors, tempera, or chalk. Listen to "The Dance of the Flowers" and draw pictures.

Week 2: Overview

Instructional Books

> *Bear's Bargain* by Frank Asch
> *Bear Shadow* by Frank Asch
> *Skyfire* by Frank Asch

Related Titles

> *Goodnight Moon* by Margaret Wise Brown
> *Papa, Please Get Me the Moon* by Eric Carle (may be read aloud)

Poems

> "Bundles" by John Farrar
> "My Shadow" by Robert Louis Stevenson

Materials

> **Teddy Grahams crackers**
>
> **Word cards for target vocabulary**

Poetry and Skills Session

DAY 1

"My Shadow"

This is a longer poem and will take more time for the children to understand.

    Step 1: After reading the whole poem, ask for general impressions.
    Step 2: Discuss shadows and how they change according to light.
    Step 3: Reread the first verse. Discuss it in more detail.

DAY 2

"My Shadow"

    Step 1: Reread the whole poem.
    Step 2: Relate the poem to *Bear Shadow*.
    Step 3: Briefly discuss the first verse, and focus on the second and third verses.
    Step 4: Introduce the vowel-plus-r combination. Tell the children than the r is a robber and steals part of the sound of vowels. To accomplish this, it must be behind the vowel. Robbers usually sneak up behind people, and that is what the r must do to get part of the sound.
    Step 5: Ask the children to locate vowel-plus-r words. Examples: *more, proper*. It will require many sessions for most children to understand this concept fully, so continue to reinforce it frequently.

DAY 3

"My Shadow"

    Step 1: Reread the poem. Allow time for general comments and discussions.
    Step 2: Encourage the children to share experiences with shadows.
    Step 3: Focus on root words during this session.

DAY 4

Bundles

The second verse of this poem contains the words "on Christmas week" in the second line. If this is changed to "during holiday weeks," the poem will be appropriate for children of all ethnic groups.

    Step 1: Read "Bundles" for the children.
    Step 2: Discuss the content. Encourage them to relate it to personal experiences. They will be able to talk about birthdays and holidays.

Step 3: Point out the use of question marks. Review their use.

Step 4: Have a box, gift wrapped if possible, containing a small treat for the children. Allow them to ask questions about what it contains. Write these questions on the board, stressing the punctuation as well as capital letters at the beginning.

Step 5: Distribute the treat.

Step 6: Reread the poem with the whole group.

DAY 5

Allow the children to select poems to read individually or with a partner. You should also make some selections.

Reading Instruction

DAY 1

Bear Shadow

Shared Reading

Step 1: Present the book to the class. Ask how it compares with other Bear books.

Step 2: Ask for predictions and write them on the board.

Step 3: Discuss the dedication.

Step 4: Read the book to the class, encouraging the children to join in as they recognize words. Provide time for discussions of the illustrations and characters as the story unfolds.

Small Group Instruction

Step 1: Mix ability groups for this session.

Step 2: Read the book together, encouraging a discussion of Bear and the story line.

Step 3: Record words that also appear in the other stories.

Step 4: Write new vocabulary words on cards. Involve the students in the selection of these words.

DAY 2

Bear Shadow

Shared Reading

Step 1: Reread the story, allowing time for comments and discussion. Guide the discussion to the things Bear has done in the various books.

Step 2: Encourage children to discuss Bear. Would they like to have him in their class. Why or why not? How does he behave like a true bear? How does he behave like a human?

Step 3: Make a bear attribute chart that includes a list of real attributes and one of fictional attributes.

Small Group Instruction

EL:

Step 1: Begin by reviewing the vocabulary from the story.

Step 2: Write some of the more difficult words on the board. Discuss ways to decode them.

Step 3: Let each child choose a word and then find a page in the book on which this word appears. Read the sentence, or the page, to the group.

TL:

Step 1: Review vocabulary words, placing difficult words on the board for decoding.

Step 2: Have the students read the story with a partner. As they read softly to each other, you can observe individuals and make note of those who need special help.

AL: Read the story silently, offering help as needed. Then ask the following questions and encourage discussion:

- Why was Bear's solution to the problem so funny?

- Do shadows really scare fish?

- How was this book like *Happy Birthday Moon?*

- How can one get rid of a shadow?

DAY 3

Skyfire

Shared Reading

Step 1: Introduce the book in the usual way, asking for predictions.

Step 2: Discuss the similarities with the other books. Read the book, pausing for comments from the class about things that are the same.

Step 3: Select vocabulary to be targeted. Write the words on pots similar to those in the story.

Small Group Instruction

Step 1: Provide copies of other Asch books. Allow the small groups to peruse the books, comparing pictures and text. If the children have not noticed, help them compare and interpret the four pictures at the bottom of the copyright and dedication pages. In each book there is a direct relationship of these pictures to the story. Encourage the pupils to speculate about the use of these pictures.

Step 2: Have the children read a book with a partner or friend.

DAY 2

Skyfire

Shared Reading

Step 1: Reread the story.

Step 2: Discuss the patterns in the story. Bear travels to another place. He talks to Bird, who is in many of the stories. He deals with aspects of nature. The children may suggest others. How do these themes compare with those in other books?

- Bear talks to the moon in *Happy Birthday Moon*.
- Bear travels to the moon in *Moongame*.
- Bear tries to get rid of his shadow in *Bear Shadow*.

Small Group Instruction

Use this time for a creative writing activity. The children are now familiar with the Bear books and will have ideas for writing. For children who have trouble finding an idea, some suggestions are as follows:

- Write a letter to Mr. Asch and ask how he gets the ideas for his books (they may also wonder about the identity of Devin).

- Write a letter to Bear and give him some advice.

- Write a description of what might happen if Bear met another bear in one of the stories.

DAY 3

Bear's Bargain

Shared Reading

Step 1: Introduce the book. Ask for predictions.

Step 2: Turn to the pages with the four small pictures of the growth of the seed. Ask for more predictions.

Step 3: Notice how the book is dedicated.

Step 4: Read the story, and discuss the accuracy of the predictions. Have the students evaluate these and conclude that, with what they know about Bear, they can make accurate guesses.

Step 5: Write vocabulary words on cards or on shapes of birds.

Small Group Instruction

Mix abilities and use directed reading questions to guide the reading. Let children work in pairs to answer questions so that the more able readers can offer support to others. Allow sentences that answer questions to be read aloud.

DAY 4

Shared Reading

Step 1: As the children read the story, ask them to look for compound words and verbs. List these as they are discovered.

Step 2: Spend time discussing with the group why Bird could not grow bigger and Bear could not fly. Does this change the way they feel about each other? This theme helps children understand that each is unique and has individual strengths.

Small Group Instruction

EL:

Step 1: Review the vocabulary with this group, playing games with the words to help them remember.

Step 2: Read the book aloud as a group. Your voice will help with words the children do not know.

Step 3: Review the use of quotation marks. Find sentences that use them.

Step 4: Working in pairs, have one child read the part of Bear or Bird and the other be the narrator.

Step 5: Let the children choose a partner and read the book for fun.

TL:

Step 1: Review the vocabulary with the group. Sort according to nouns, verbs, and adjectives.

Step 2: Review the use of quotation marks.

Step 3: Read the book aloud as a play, with students taking the part of Bear, Bird, and narrator of the book.

AL:

Step 1: Ask the children to read the book silently. Give assistance where needed.

Step 2: Encourage the children to discuss why Bear and Bird want to be something they are not. What is the difference between animals and humans learning things that are not natural? Example: People wanted to fly, so the airplane was invented. Could animals accomplish anything like this? What about the tricks animals perform? Is there something the children in the group would like to do that seems to be impossible? Will it ever be possible?

DAY 5

Shared Reading

- Plan a bear party for reading time. Ask the children to dress a bear like a character from their favorite book and bring both bear and book to school. Allow time for the stories to be shared with the class. Have each child read or tell, depending on the child, one of the Bear stories to their bear.

- Have students draw a favorite scene from one of the stories and tell the class about it.

- Ask the children what games might be played at the party (for example: pin the tail on the bear). They might think of other games adaptable to a bear theme.

- Provide some sort of bear snack as part of the party. Teddy Grahams are a healthful and inexpensive treat. Bread and honey would also be appropriate.

- Encourage children to evaluate the Bear books. Did they enjoy reading them? What was the most fun? Was there a part they did not like? Accepting these comments will provide insight into strategies that motivate children.

Independent Activities

Materials

12-by-18-inch manila paper

Construction paper in rainbow colors

Small pot (like the mythical one at the end of the rainbow)

Paper sacks or other puppet material

Heavy drawing paper

Business-size envelopes, one per child

Extension Activities

- The moon and sun are used frequently in the Bear stories. Have the children fold a piece of 12-by-18-inch paper in half. On one side write "Moon," on the other write "Sun." Write words or phrases associated with each on the appropriate half. Examples: *Sun: hot, shadows, day, summer. Moon: night, half, new, stars.*

- Suggest that a rainbow has suddenly formed in the sky outside the school and ended on the playground. The children can see the pot of treasure that is supposed to be at the end. Have them write a story about this treasure and what they would do with it.

- A variation on this idea is to bring a pot or similar container to the class and tell the children it was found at the end of a rainbow. Ask them to write a story about what was in it. They can extend this idea by telling what happened to the treasure. This story can be written in a pot- or rainbow-shaped book.

- "Bear" is a good word for rhyming. Children may enjoy working in pairs or small groups to write poems about bears, to be shared with others in the class. This might be the beginning of a poetry book written by the class. Encourage children to add to this book throughout the year. At the end of the year, it might be presented to the school library.

Small Group and Center Activities

- Make a rainbow to hang on a Christmas tree. Place a variety of rainbow-colored construction paper on a table. Have the children cut out the shape of a rainbow from a piece of firm paper, such as tag board, and cut strips of colored paper to glue on their rainbow.

- Use paper bags to make puppets of the characters in *The Nutcracker*. Allow time for the creation and performance of a short play about the story.

- Draw individual pictures about *The Nutcracker* or one of the Bear stories on heavy paper. Laminate them and have the children cut their pictures into puzzle pieces. Place the pieces in a decorated envelope. These can be used as gifts for younger children.

Science

- Continue the study of bears, presenting any material that was not covered during the previous week.

- Use the individual maps the children worked with during the previous units to have them locate homes of the various bears.

- Discuss food, habits, and how bears have adapted to the changes in their environments. The need for protection of their homes should be stressed.

- Make a true-and-false list of ideas about bears found in literature. The children will be familiar with many of these stories and can analyze them for this purpose.

Math

- Have the children write story problems about bears and read them to a partner. The partner writes a number sentence that reflects the problem and then takes a turn with his or her story.

- Conduct a survey to determine the most popular color for teddy bears. Make a graph to show the results.

- Determine how many children it would take to match the weight of the sun bear. Assume that each child weighs approximately fifty pounds. This can lead to a discussion on approximation.

Foreign Language

Begin using holiday words in the language being studied. If a foreign language teacher is on the faculty, enlist help in discussing the customs of the country or countries in which the language is spoken. Connect this to the social studies unit.

Music

Continue listening to *The Nutcracker*. Highlight various movements, and encourage the children to verbalize their feelings about the music.

Art

Make fingerprint pictures of bears. One print forms the body and others make the head, arms, and legs. Use a marker to add ears, eyes, and nose. Add a background. These can be laminated and will make a nice gift for parents. The fingerprint can also be used as the basis for a character from *The Nutcracker*.

Week 3: Overview

Instructional Books

The Twelve Days of Christmas folksong
The Nutcracker retold by Pat Whitehead

Related Titles

The Little Fir Tree by Margaret Wise Brown (to be read aloud)
The Story of the Nutcracker Ballet by Deborah Hautiz (to be read aloud)
Herschel and the Hanukkah Goblins by Eric Kimmel (to be read aloud)
Favorite Stories of the Ballet by James Riordan (to be read aloud)
How the Grinch Stole Christmas by Dr. Seuss (to be read aloud)

Videocassettes

The Nutcracker. American Ballet Theater Video Tape

Poems

"Merry Christmas" by Aileen Fisher
"Hanukkah Rainbow" by Eva Grant
"Paper 1" by Carl Sandburg

Objectives

1. **Phonetic skills**
   Review vowels followed by r.
   Identify and read vowel digraphs ou and ow.

2. **Structural analysis**
   Review and apply decoding skills.

3. **Punctuation**
   Review the use of quotation marks.

Materials

Word cards in shapes related to The Nutcracker and "The Twelve Days of Christmas"

Paper for creative writing

Art paper for illustrations

Poetry and Skills Session

DAY 1

"Paper 1"

Step 1: Introduce the poem through a discussion of gift paper. Ask the children to think of the most beautifully wrapped gift they ever received. Allow time to describe the wrapping.

Step 2: Follow with a discussion of other kinds of paper.

Step 3: Point out that the poem they are reading talks about two kinds of paper. Read the poem together and identify the kinds of paper.

Step 4: This poem is excellent for teaching the wr blend. Have the children mark the words that begin with these letters. Listen to the sound, and list other words that begin with them.

Step 5: Read the poem again for pleasure.

DAY 2

"Merry Christmas"

Step 1: Read the poem together. Discuss the meaning.

Step 2: What would the words look like in the snow if a mouse had made them with its feet? Encourage children to have fun with this idea.

Step 3: Identify the ou and ow words. Listen for the sounds made by these vowel digraphs. List other words that contain the sounds.

Step 4: Read the poem again.

Step 5: Distribute copies of the poem for your students to illustrate and include in their poetry notebooks.

DAY 3

"Merry Christmas"

Step 1: Reread "Merry Christmas." Identify the rhyming words.

Step 2: How could the word "mouse" be changed to another animal? What would be used instead of "house"? Encourage students to create variations of the poem in this manner.

DAY 4

"Hanukkah Rainbow"

Step 1: Introduce this poem by asking students of the Jewish faith to share the importance of candles in their holiday celebrations.

Step 2: Encourage someone in the class to talk about the importance of the menorah in the celebration of Hanukkah. (This should correspond with the focus on Israel in the social studies unit.)

Step 3: Read the poem together. Interpret the meaning.

Step 4: Identify the adjectives, noting how they give color to the poem.

DAY 5

Read individual choices for pleasure.

Reading Instruction

The Nutcracker

This week will probably precede winter break; therefore the suggestions for reading are grouped by individual books rather by day. This should offer more flexibility in planning at this busy time. The following are questions and activities appropriate to *The Nutcracker*.

Shared Reading

Step 1: Read the book to the class. Because the text is difficult, it will be used independently with the more advanced readers, although the entire class will enjoy the story.

Step 2: Relate the story to the music played during this month. Play the various movements and connect them to the story. This is most effective when presented over several days.

Small Group Instruction

This story has many difficult words; the children should not be expected to master all of them. Use directed reading strategies, offering support as needed.

- Encourage the children to begin a list of new words. Examples: *glittered, Herr, Drosselmeyer, fierce,* and *magnificent*. Be sure the students understand the meanings. These words can be written on paper, illustrated, and combined to make a vocabulary book.

- Choose a character from the story, draw a picture of it, and write a few sentences about it.

- Parts of the story are frightening. Discuss them.

- Ask the children what they would do if they were suddenly in the Land of Sweets. What would they expect to find there? Have them draw a picture and write a few sentences about it.

- The Sugar Plum Fairy evokes many images. Ask the students what words they would use to describe her. These words should be recorded on the board as the suggestions are made. They can be used for writing activities at another time.

- Compare different versions of the story.

- Show *The Nutcracker* video produced by The American Ballet Theater.

The Twelve Days of Christmas

Shared Reading

Step 1: Have a recording of this song available, and have the class sing along. Write the words on chart paper so the class can read as they sing.

Step 2: The words from each verse can be written on sheets of paper and combined into a book. This can be of student size or a large class big book.

Step 3: Ask the children to illustrate the verses.

Small Group Instruction

- Make word cards of the characters and numbers in the song. Have the children match them.

- Write phrases from the song on the word cards. Have the children sequence them. Examples: *six geese, five gold rings.*

- The words will be familiar to the children after a few days, so allow plenty of opportunity for them to read to someone. If possible, go to a younger class and have the children read the story to a friend. This will be most effective if it is one-on-one rather than one child reading to a whole group.

- Create a play, using the students' pictures and the lyrics of the song.

- Enjoy the absurdity of this song by helping the children imagine someone actually giving another these gifts. What would one do with eight maids a-milking or ten lords a-leaping? The children might enjoy acting out the story.

- Compare other book versions of the song.

Independent Activities

Materials

Red and green construction paper in 3-by-11-inch strips

Cards with one to twelve items drawn on them

Cards on which the number words "one" to "twelve" are written

Twelve small boxes, gift wrapped

12-by-18-inch white art paper

Extension Activities

- Have students make a sequence chain of the events in *The Nutcracker* or *The Twelve Days of Christmas,* using red and green construction paper. Encourage them to work in pairs.

- The Mouse King is not a sympathetic character in the book. What could one do to help him learn to be a better example to his followers? Have students write about it.

- The person giving the gifts in the song had a hard time thinking of things to give. Ask the students to name twelve gifts that would be appropriate for a friend or family member.

Small Group and Center Activities

- Make a set of cards with one to twelve items on them. Provide a set with the numbers 1 to 12 and another with the words "one" to "twelve." Place these in a center for matching.

- Place copies of the book and a tape of the song at a listening center. The students will enjoy listening to the tape and following the text in the books.

- Gift wrap twelve small boxes (earring boxes are a good size). Place them in a larger container. Have the children arrange the boxes in equal groups. How many sets can they devise? Examples: two sets of six; six sets of two. Provide paper on which they can record their findings. It will help if lines have been drawn to divide the paper into boxes and " _____ sets of _____ " is written at the bottom of each box.

- Fold a sheet of 12-by-18-inch paper in half and in half again. Repeat this three more times. This creates a page with 32 boxes. Direct the children to write their initials in the first box. Choosing two symbols of the season (wreath, candle, star, or tree), they are to draw one in each of the next two boxes and then repeat this pattern of three in the rest of the boxes on the page. In lieu of drawing, tempera and stamps made from potatoes could be used. The repeated design creates custom-made wrapping paper. Have the children use this to wrap one of their gifts. Encourage the students to complete this over several days. The more care taken, the more lovely the results.

Social Studies

Objectives

1. **Map skills**
   Review the location of countries previously introduced: Mexico, Israel, England, Germany, France, Russia, Italy, and Spain.
2. **Learn about the holiday customs of the preceding countries.**
3. **Holiday Customs around the World**

Religion is the basis of this unit because of the nature of the celebrations. However, it should be handled from a historical perspective and as the primary influence on the formation of customs. The primary focus should be *how* the holidays are observed rather than *why*. One of the goals of this study is to foster a greater understanding of and respect for the differences among the people who inhabit our world.

The Nutcracker is an essential part of the curriculum during this month. Each day when the children are arriving, and when appropriate during the day, play this music. Any book about this ballet will provide the background needed. It is assumed that most schedules do not allow time for a social studies lesson each day; therefore three a week are suggested. All lessons are grouped rather than being listed by the week, thus making it easier to implement the unit. The sessions may be extended or shortened to complement the individual class schedule.

In preparation for this unit, survey the parents of the class and ask for information about how December holidays are observed in their homes. Suggested questions are as follows:

- Does your family have a special custom that is included in your holiday celebrations?

- Does this custom originate in another country?

- Do you have a relative or friend who might be willing to share customs of other countries with our class?

People connected with churches, colleges, libraries, and ethnic clubs are often willing to speak to young children about customs unique to a particular country. They can offer firsthand information and help children relate to these cultures. As often as possible, provide a taste of food associated with the country or custom under discussion.

Russia: *S Rozhestvom Khristovym*

Using a map or globe, compare the location of Russia to that of France, England, the United States, and the home town of the class. Ask what can the class infer about weather and means of travel to Russia.

Read the story of *The Nutcracker*. Encourage students to bring any nutcrackers they may have to class. Allow time for children to share their knowledge of this ballet. Identify and list various characters in the ballet: Fritz, Marie, Godpapa Drosselmeyer, Nutcracker, Mice, Soldiers, Prince, Sugar Plum Fairy, and Russian Dancers.

Discuss the movements of the Russian dance. Play this part of the ballet. If there is a music teacher available, a cooperative lesson could include other music typical of Russia.

Discuss the customs of Russia. Because of the recent history of Russia, few customs are associated with this time of the year. One story tells about an old woman, "Babushka," who brought gifts, leaving them under the pillow while the children slept.

Israel

Hanukkah is usually celebrated during the first part of December and should be included at the proper time. Arrange for someone to tell the children the story of Hanukkah. Discuss the meaning of the menorah and the symbolism of the candles. Read "Hanukkah Rainbow" with the children.

Locate Israel on the map. Encourage discussion of the history of this country. Introduce the dreidel, and teach the children how to play the game using gelt. Ask someone to make latkes for the children. These can be made at home and brought to the class. They are usually served with applesauce.

Germany: *Fröhliche Weinachten*

The Christmas tree originated in Germany. Read *The Little Fir Tree* to the children. The traditional German Christmas tree is decorated with candles. This offers a good opportunity to bring in a brief safety lesson with questions about how these customs are modified for present-day use. Gift giving is associated with both St. Nicholas and Kris Kringle.

Mexico: *Feliz Navidad*

Although Mexico is not represented in *The Nutcracker,* it is a country that should be included in this study because of the traditions that have become part of the holiday. The observance begins on December 16 with a re-enactment of the journey of Mary and Joseph looking for shelter. Each night the people look for a place. Finally, on the evening of the 24th, a resting place is found. This religious custom is followed by a party with games and a piñata. The children receive their gifts on January 6.

The poinsettia was introduced to the United States by Ambassador to Mexico Dr. Joel Roberts Poinsett in 1825. He sent cuttings of the flower to Philadelphia. In areas of the southwestern United States where American Indian traditions have become intertwined with Mexican ones, luminarias line roofs, walks, and fences on Christmas Eve.

England: *Merry Christmas*

The tradition of the Christmas tree was brought to England during the reign of Queen Victoria by her husband, Prince Albert. The origin of the Christmas card is attributed to Sir Henry Cole, who tried to avoid writing greetings to his friends (Hildebrand, N. D.). Plum pudding, mince pie, and the wassail bowl are traditional foods that can be traced to the English.

Because soldiers are associated with the changing of the guard, children enjoy using this link between England and *The Nutcracker*.

France: *Joyeux Noel*

The yule log was part of the French tradition and served as the center of the family celebrations. After it had burned, the ashes were often sprinkled around plants. As a substitute for burning the yule log, people began baking a cake shaped like a log. It was covered with chocolate frosting to look like bark.

Gifts were brought to the children by Le Père Noël, Father Christmas. He was accompanied by Father Spanker who "rewarded" bad children. Adults receive their gifts on New Year's Day.

Italy: *Buon Natale*

The holiday in Italy is religious. It centers around the church and the season of Advent. The children look forward to the Feast of Epiphany on January 6. They hang stockings in anticipation of a visit from Befana, a kind of female Santa Claus. The legend is that she declined an offer by the Wise Men to accompany them as they paid their respects to Jesus. She later realized her mistake and now spends the night of January 5 looking for the Baby, leaving gifts for children during her search.

Spain: *Felices Pascuas*

Following midnight mass on Christmas Eve, the people in Spain begin celebrating with dancing and singing in the streets. In Spain, as in Italy, the big day for children is January 6. The legend is that the Wise Men travel through the towns each year. The children leave straw in their shoes for the camels, and it is replaced with gifts.

Independent Activities

Materials

Drawing paper

Green construction paper cut into large triangles, two per child

Craft sticks, two per child

Colored yarn

Small brown paper sacks

Newspaper, cut into strips

Liquid starch

Balloons

Colored tissue paper

12-by-18-inch white construction paper

Large wooden beads

Pipe cleaners

Net or plastic, cut into strips

- As children listen to the music of *The Nutcracker,* have them draw or paint a picture of what they hear. "The Waltz of the Flowers" and "Dance of the Sugar Plum Fairy" are especially appropriate for this activity.

- Cut two large triangles of green construction paper. Cut from the point halfway down on one, and from the bottom halfway up on the second. These will then fit together to form a tree. Children can decorate the tree with small ornaments and tiny paper chains made of construction paper or even small strings of popcorn.

- Glue two craft sticks together to form a + . Cut a piece of variegated colored yarn about three feet long. Glue one end to the center of the sticks and wrap it around the sticks to make a god's eye.

- Make a luminaria by cutting a design in a small brown paper sack. Put approximately two cups of sand in the bottom. Place a tea light in the center. When lighted, the candle will highlight the cut design. Caution children to put this in a safe place to avoid the danger of fire.

- Children can make a piñata by dipping strips of newspaper into a liquid starch solution and covering an inflated balloon with them. After the papier-mâché has dried, cut a hole in the top, add candy, and add a second layer of colored tissue paper covering the hole.

- To make a soldier, fold a piece of 12-by-18-inch manila construction paper in half, leaving a small edge on one side to form a lip for gluing. Fold again, creating four equal rectangles. When glued together, it forms a long "box" with open ends. Allow the children to see the final shape, but do not glue it until it has been colored. On one section draw the front of the soldier. The two connecting panels become the sides, and the remaining panel is the back. Strips of metallic paper can form a belt, buttons, or decorations on the uniform or hat. Wooden ice cream spoons can be glued to the sides to make arms.

- A sugar plum fairy can be made from a large bead, two long pipe cleaners, and some netting or plastic (such as a bag from the dry cleaner) or construction paper. Put the pipe cleaners through the hole in the bead, and shape arms and legs. Using an ink pen, draw a face on the bead. The skirt can be made from strips of netting or plastic, 2 1/2-by-12-inch. Using a needle, draw a long line of thread through one edge of the material and pull tightly, gathering it into a skirt. Anchor it to the pipe cleaners with the end of the gathering thread. (*A New Look at Christmas Decorations* by Sister M. Gratia Listaite and Norbert A. Hildebrand was very helpful in the preparation of this section.)

Science

Step 1: Complete the study of bears during this week. Encourage students to add a final page that summarizes what they have learned about bears and their feelings about the unit.

Step 2: Assemble the book of bears, and have the children design a cover.

Step 3: Allow time for the students to share their books with the group. Conduct a general discussion about things they have learned.

Note: Use the books and the discussion as an evaluation tool for science.

Math

"The Twelve Days of Christmas" offers a wide variety of activities for math:

- Make a book of the songs illustrating each verse. Write a number sentence for each number at the bottom of that page.

- Every verse repeats each item previously mentioned. If "five gold rings" were presented on days 5 through 12, how many would be given in all? This could be done with each gift. Choose one item and then show the solution to the problem.

- Assuming that each item is presented only on the correspondingly numbered day (six geese a-laying only on day 6), how many things in all were given? Show the solution.

- Learn to read and perhaps spell the number words.

- Twelve is referred to as "a dozen." How many things are sold in this quantity. Make a class list.

Foreign Language

Names of the characters in *The Nutcracker* can be introduced in the foreign language being studied. Discuss the words from the music that have a base in other languages. Count to twelve in the language. Review and evaluate the words introduced during this study.

Music

Listen to and sing "The Twelve Days of Christmas." Using pictures drawn during the week, act out the song. Show the video of the American Ballet Theater presentation of *The Nutcracker*. This is a long tape, approximately 90 minutes, so it would be best to divide it into two or three sessions.

Art

- Draw a picture of the Land of Sweets from *The Nutcracker*. Paint over the picture with pink water colors. This produces a fairylike picture.

- Assemble the book of bears. Have the children design a cover made of construction paper.

- Cut a large tree from a piece of 12-by-18-inch green construction paper. (It may be helpful for the children to have a pattern to follow.) Dip small pieces of sponge in colored paint and decorate the tree. Make small paper chains from 3-by-1 1/2-inch strips of colored paper; glue them on the tree. Encourage the children to use their own ideas to decorate the tree. Glue the finished tree on a red sheet. This can be stapled to a second piece of paper. The children can use it as a container in which to carry home the holiday work they have created. For children who do not celebrate Christmas, use a large candle, menorah, or other symbol of their choosing.

Bibliography

Books

Asch, Frank. *Happy Birthday Moon*. New York: Scholastic, 1982.
———. *Mooncake*. New York: Scholastic, 1987.
———. *Moongame*. New York: Scholastic, 1989.
———. *Bear Shadow*. New York: Scholastic, 1990a.
———. *Skyfire*. New York: Scholastic, 1990b.
———. *Bear's Bargain*. New York: Scholastic, 1991.
Brown, Margaret Wise. *Goodnight Moon*. New York: Scholastic, 1947.
———. *The Little Fir Tree*. New York: Thomas Y. Crowell, 1985.
Carle, Eric. *Papa, Please Get Me the Moon*. New York: Scholastic, 1990.
Freeman, Don. *Corduroy*. New York: Viking, 1968.
Hautzig, Deborah. *The Story of the Nutcracker Ballet*. New York: Random House, 1986.
Jeunesse, Gallimard, and Laura Bour. *Bears: A First Discovery Book*. New York: Scholastic, 1992.
Kimmel, Eric. *Hershel and the Hanukkah Goblins*. New York: Scholastic, 1990.
The Nutcracker. Retold by Pat Whitehead. Mahwah, N.J.: Troll Associates, 1988.
Riordan, James. *Favorite Stories of the Ballet*. Chicago: Rand McNally, 1986.
Seuss, Dr. *How the Grinch Stole Christmas*. New York: Random House, 1957.

The Twelve Days of Christmas. Illustrated by Susan Swan. Mahwah, N.J.: Troll Associates, 1981.

Van Allsburg, Chris. *Polar Express.* Boston: Houghton, Mifflin, 1985.

Poems

Austin, Mary. "Grizzly Bear." In *The Sound of Poetry,* edited by Mary C. Austin and Queenie B. Mills. Boston: Allyn and Bacon, 1963.

Farrar, John. "Bundles." In *Time for Poetry*, edited by May Hill Arbuthnot. Chicago: Scott, Foresman, 1951.

Fisher, Aileen. "Merry Christmas." In *The Random House Book of Poetry for Children,* edited by Jack Prelutsky. New York: Random House, 1983.

Grant, Eva. "Hanukkah Rainbow." In *Poetry Place Anthology,* edited by Rosemary Alexander. New York: Scholastic, 1983.

Sandburg, Carl. "Paper 1." In *Poetry Place Anthology,* edited by Rosemary Alexander. New York: Scholastic, 1983.

Sendak, Maurice. "December." In *Chicken Soup with Rice,* Maurice Sendak. New York: Scholastic, 1987.

Stevenson, Robert L. "My Shadow." In *The Sound of Poetry,* edited by Mary C. Austin and Queenie B. Mills. Boston: Allyn and Bacon, 1963.

Yolen, Jane. "Grandpa Bear's Lullaby." In *Sing a Song of Popcorn,* edited by Beatrice de Regniers, Eva Moore, Mary Michaels White, and Jan Carr. New York: Scholastic, 1988.

References

deMontreville, Doris, and Elizabeth D. Crawford, eds. *Fourth Book of Junior Authors and Illustrators.* New York: H. H. Wilson, 1978.

Listaite, M. Gratia, and Norbert A. Hildebrand. *A New Look at Christmas Decorations.* Milwaukee: Bruce Publishing, N.D.

Stirling, Ian. *Sierra Club Wildlife Library: Bears.* San Francisco: Sierra Club Books for Children, 1992.

2
JANUARY

Theme: Let It Snow in January

January brings the snow and, along with it, *The Snowy Day,* by January author of the month, Ezra Jack Keats. This month's winter theme incorporates a unit on winter birds as the science connection and a study of Rimsky-Korsakov's ballet opera, *Snow Maiden.*

Week 1: Overview

Instructional Book

The Snowy Day by Ezra Jack Keats

Related Titles

The Snowman by Raymond Briggs (picture book)
The Snowman Storybook by Raymond Briggs (to be read aloud)
January Brings the Snow by Sara Coleridge (to be read aloud)
The Snowman Who Went for a Walk by Mira Lobe (to be read aloud)
Snow Day by Betty Mastro (to be read aloud)
Sadie and the Snowman by Allen Morgan (to be read aloud)

Poems

"First Snow" by Marie Lousie Allen
"Snow" by Karla Kuskin
"January" by Maurice Sendak
"Sh" by James S. Tippett

Music

"Dance of the Clowns" from *Snow Maiden* by Rimsky-Korsakov.

Video

The Snowman by Snowman Enterprises

Objectives

1. **Phonetic skills**
   Begin to understand consonant digraphs sh, ch, th, wh, sn, and st.

2. **Structural analysis**
   Begin to understand plural and possessive nouns.
   Begin to understand apostrophes.
   Review the concept of compound words.

3. **Comprehension**
   Review the concepts of comparing and contrasting.

Materials

Word cards in the shape of a snowman or snowflake

White paper

Poetry and Skills Session

DAY 1

"January"

Step 1: Read the poem to the class, allowing them to join in on the last four lines.

Step 2: Ask why sipping hot soup in January would be nice.

Step 3: Identify nouns, verbs, and adjectives during these sessions for the rest of the week.

Step 4: Identify long and short vowel words.

Step 5: Identify the contraction "it's."

DAY 2

"Sh"

Step 1: Read the poem with the children several times, enjoying the rhythm of it.

Step 2: Have the children interpret the poem and identify and describe Mrs. Grumpy Grundy.

Step 3: Teach the digraph sh. Explain consonant blends.

Step 4: Ask the children to think of other words containing sh sounds. Write them on chart paper. Encourage the students to try to think of words with sh at the beginning, in the middle, and at the end.

Step 5: James S. Tippet wrote many poems about the city and about children who live in the city. Compare the writing of Tippet and Keats.

DAY 3

"Snow"

Time constraints may preclude the use of all of these activities in one session. Use them as appropriate to individual schedules and to the attention span of the group.

Step 1: Review all poetry introduced during the week by doing a choral reading of each poem.

Step 2: With erasable pens, have the children draw a red circle around nouns, a blue circle around verbs, and a green circle around adjectives. Do each separately.

Step 3: Focus on vowel sounds that need reteaching, and ask the children to find examples in the poem.

Step 4: As the poetry is read, clap on nouns, snap fingers on adjectives, and stand up or hop on verbs. (This reinforces the concept of doing.)

Step 5: Introduce "Snow." Read it aloud as a group.

Step 6: Review the sh sound.

Step 7: Introduce the digraphs ch, th, and wh. Identify them in the poetry. Begin making lists of words that have the sounds.

DAY 4

"First Snow"

Step 1: Review the poetry and skills from days 1, 2, and 3.

Step 2: Introduce "First Snow." Discuss the simile in the poem, and ask the children to find examples in other poems in their notebooks.

Step 3: Discuss the function of s at the end of a word to make it plural: Examples: *bush - bushes* (in this case es), *ball - balls*, and *place - places*. Find plural nouns in other poems.

Step 4: Review wh. Examples: *whiteness, where,* and *somewhere.*

Step 5: Find examples of sh, ch, sn, and st in the poem.

DAY 5

Read the poetry for pleasure.

Reading Instruction

DAY 1

Biographical sketch of Ezra Jack Keats

Ezra Keats was the son of Polish immigrants. He was born in Brooklyn, New York, on March 11, 1916, and died on May 6, 1983. As a young child, he loved to draw on any flat surface. Once he drew on the top of the kitchen table. He thought his mother would be cross and tell him to clean the surface. Instead she covered it with a cloth and when neighbors visited she removed the cloth to show her son's work (Kovacs and Preller, 1991).

Although he did not wish his son to pursue a career in art, Mr. Keats recognized his son's talent. One day, Mr. Keats came home and said, "If you don't think artists starve, well, let me tell you. One man came in the other day and swapped me a tube of paint for a bowl of soup." Ezra's father put down a brand-new tube of paint (Commire 1977, 81). Mr. Keats continued to "swap" for paint until it became obvious to the young artist that his father was actually buying the paint. Upon his father's death, Ezra discovered that he carried in his wallet the newspaper clippings telling of the awards his son had won. His father was proud of Ezra's talent but never resolved the fear that Ezra would not be able to support himself.

Ezra Keats won several scholarships to art school but was unable to accept them because it was during the Depression and he had to work to support his family. He taught himself to paint using a variety of materials. Collage became one of his favorite mediums. He felt it was a way to fuse shapes and colors and balance reality and illusion (Commire 1977).

He also wrote stories, and many of his stories are based on experiences from his childhood. He began to illustrate books, as well, but was bothered because he was never asked to illustrate stories about black children. He decided to write *The Snowy Day*, in which he would show the beauty and goodness of black children (Kovacs and Preller 1991).

Ezra Keats never became a parent, but he felt that the characters in his books were his children. He was captivated by some photographs he saw in a magazine and kept them for many years. They became the inspiration for Peter. Children read his books and identify with the characters. They would often write to him (Norby and Ryan 1988).

The Snowy Day

Shared Reading

Step 1: Before predicting the story from the cover of *The Snowy Day* big book, ask the class to think of things they can do outside on a snowy day. Ask them how they feel when they are out in the snow. Have them close their eyes and think of adjectives to describe snow. (If the school is in an area that does not get snow, help the children locate snow areas on the map. Pretending will be great fun, and they will enjoy the snow activities even more.)

Step 2: Read *The Snowy Day* together.

Step 3: Ask the following questions: Where do you think Peter lives? Why? What kind of house does Peter live in? Why? Lead the students to conclude that Peter lives in an apartment house in the city. Ask students to find a sentence in the book that supports this. (The last page of the book has the information.)

Step 4: As this discussion progresses, introduce author Ezra Jack Keats. The children probably noticed Peter and identified him as a black child. Tell them that Ezra Jack Keats grew up in a tough neighborhood and many of the children in his stories are black. Most of his stories are set in the city as well. Read the biography of Mr. Keats to the class.

Small Group Instruction

Because the shared reading session covered so much material and was probably extended, forgo small group instruction today. If the children are eager to do more, let them look at the student copies in pairs.

DAY 2

The Snowy Day

Shared Reading

Step 1: Read *The Snowy Day* aloud as a group.

Step 2: Ask the children to examine the illustrations carefully. How do they think Mr. Keats made the pictures? Help them to recognize the technique as collage and compare it with Eric Carle's work.

Step 3: As the children are guided through the book, ask what they think the illustrator used to make specific pictures and how he used the material (torn-paper technique, tissue paper, and wallpaper). Call attention to the backgrounds, and ask how Mr. Keats achieved the repeated use of patterns.

Step 4: Remind the class that Keats' family was very poor and, although he displayed artistic talent at a young age, they had no money to buy paper. Once he drew pictures all over an enamel kitchen table. Instead of washing his pictures off the table, his mother covered the table with a cloth and proudly showed his work to all her neighbors. Ask what their mothers would do or say if they drew pictures on the kitchen table.

Small Group Instruction

Step 1: Mix the abilities for today's work. Use guided reading strategies. Have the group read the story and locate the answers to questions on each page. Suggest key words in the questions so the less independent readers will have success.

Step 2: Have the children choose from the story words that they think are difficult and write them on mitten-shaped word cards.

Step 3: Arrange the cards in alphabetical order.

Step 4: Identify words in the story that have the sh, ch, and wh sounds.

DAY 3

The Snowy Day

Shared Reading

Step 1: Reread *The Snowy Day*, with small groups alternately reading the pages.

Step 2: Discuss Mr. Keats' life as a child. Ask how Keats' childhood was similar to and different from their own.

Step 3: Ask whether Mr. Keats' childhood could have been like Peter's. Have the children explain their answers.

Step 4: Ask what Peter did in the snow that would be fun for the children? Would the class like to have Peter for a friend? Why or why not?

Step 5: Discuss the part of the story in which Peter put a snowball in his pocket to save it. Could he have guessed what would happen? Why did he put it there? How could he have saved his snowball?

Step 6: On chart paper, write a list of winter words suggested by the children. Have the children illustrate the words on the chart. Display this as a picture dictionary for the class.

Small Group Instruction

Step 1: Find the compound words that have *snow* as part of the word. Encourage the children to think of more compound words that can be made with *snow*. Expand the list to other compound words from the story and words from the children's experience.

Step 2: Explore root words and endings in the story. Draw a tree on the board showing an elaborate root system. Explain that roots hold the tree in the ground and without them the tree could not stand tall and straight. Compare the root of the word to the roots of the tree. The root word holds the word up and helps it to have meaning. Have the children suggest words to add to the tree. Example: *walk, walking,* and *walked.*

Step 3: Ask the group to make a list of five words from the story that have endings. Show the root word. Use both the root word and the word with an ending in separate sentences. The objective is to help the children see how the ending changes the use of the word. This can be done as a paper-and-pencil activity or orally, depending upon time and the maturity of the group.

DAY 4

The Snowman

Shared Reading

Step 1: Discuss all of the things Peter did in the snow. Encourage the children to identify Peter's activities with their own. Give everyone a chance to share their experiences.

Step 2: Someone will surely mention building a snowman, just like Peter. Use this discussion as an introduction to Raymond Briggs' wordless picture book, *The Snowman*. Go through the book with the children, encouraging them to express their creative ideas about what is happening in the illustrations. Invite them to add a bit of "serendipity" to their accounts of the action.

Note: After this session, find a time to show the children the delightful video, *The Snowman*. The music that accompanies the action is especially appropriate and beautiful.

Small Group Instruction

With the wordless version of *The Snowman* on hand, help each instructional group begin a cooperative chart story based on the book or a part of the book, with you acting as scribe. Involve the children in the spelling of the words whenever possible. For example, if someone tells the snowman to be quiet as he enters the house, ask them what letters they know that spell "sh." If they decide to have lunch, ask them to supply the short u and the digraph ch.

Although the stories may be completed in one session, plan to use the small group instructional time during the next session for further work.

DAY 5

The Snowman Storybook

Shared Reading

Note: Big book versions of *The Snowman Storybook* are not available at this time. It is helpful for you to make a large copy for use with the class. This version contains simple text, which should be included with the illustrations. For use in small-group instruction, it is helpful for each student to have a copy.

Step 1: Read the storybook to the children (or read it with them if a large copy has been made).

Step 2: Compare and contrast the different versions of the story.

Step 3: Compare this story with the ones the children wrote in the small groups.

Step 4: Encourage the children to identify the Briggs books as fantasy. Then ask them what things in the book could really happen.

Small Group Instruction

Step 1: If necessary, complete the cooperative snowman stories begun the previous day. Read the stories together. Provide an opportunity to discuss and critique each group's work. Set some ground rules with the class to help the children learn how to criticize, give praise, and make suggestions to each other.

Step 2: When the group stories are completed, make individual copies for the children to illustrate. The stories can be made into small books for them to read together and then take home.

Independent Activities

Materials

Patterns for circles: small, medium, and large

Construction paper for scarf, mittens, and so on, for snowman

Paper for folded or flip books

Snowman-shaped books for student writing activity

Extension Activities

- Write a name poem about snow, then illustrate it. Example:

  Snow fell softly on a winter morning.
  Not a sound could be heard as the snow covered the ground.
  One by one the children came outside to play
  We had a wonderful day playing in the snow.

  Other options can include the following:

  A name poem using the letters of the child's first name
  A name poem using a winter word

- On folded paper or on flip books, illustrate vocabulary or phrases from *The Snowy Day* and *The Snowman Storybook*.

- Write sentences using *The Snowy Day* vocabulary cards.

- Encourage the children to rewrite *The Snowy Day,* telling of another adventure Peter and a friend might have had.

- Rewrite the ending of *The Snowy Day.*

- Using cut paper, have each child make a creative snowman - no crayons or pencils, please! This may require two sessions to complete.

Session 1

Suggest that the children choose a place they would like to visit with a snowman friend. Provide each group of four children with three cardboard circles to use as patterns for the body of their snowman (small for the head, medium for the midsection, large for the lower body). Trace the circles on white paper. Then cut out and glue them together to shape the snowman. (You may prefer to have the children cut freehand circles. This works, too. However, a few children will end up with snowmen so small they won't be able to add details.) Ask the children to decide where they are going with their snow friend and to add details accordingly. Example: A child planning to go skiing with the snowman might add a tassel cap or earmuffs, mittens, and a pair of skis. They should also add the facial features, buttons, arms, and any other detail they wish. The result of this activity is a group of whimsical snow people that really motivate creative writing.

Session 2

The next day, or at least during another period, ask the children to write a story to go along with their snowman. Mutually agree that the story should include the following:

Where you are going
How you will get there
What you will do together after you arrive
How to get back home or another appropriate ending

These guidelines should be written on the chalkboard so the class can refer to them as they write the story. The stories may then be written in snowman-shaped books and illustrated. This extension activity may take several days to complete. The snow people and stories can be shared with a younger class and then displayed on a large bulletin board.

- Have the children complete a literature report on *The Snowy Day* or *The Snowman Storybook* (see form on p. 43). The report form is self-explanatory, but the children should be guided through the first one. "I think . . . " should be the start of the child's evaluation of the book, of who they think should read the book and why, and of any other comments they would like to make. Encourage the use of colorful words instead of "The illustrations were nice," or "Peter was nice."

Literature Report

Name

Book

Author

Illustrator

Characters:

Setting:

1.

2.

3.

Small Group and Center Activities

Note: Session 1 in the preceding subsection, making the creative snowman, adapts well to centers.

- Fold a piece of dark blue 9-by-12-inch construction paper in half to make a booklet. Staple a piece of handwriting paper inside. On one side, the children are to write "Winter is . . . " and on the other side, "Snow is . . . " They are to write as many adjectives as they can to finish each sentence stem. On the front, they can glue a creative snowflake cut from a square or circle of white paper. The snowflake can be outlined with glue and sprinkled with glitter to make it sparkle. The work with the glue and glitter can be a center activity.

- Write and illustrate a winter story in a large mitten-shaped book.

- Based on *The Snowy Day* or one of the group stories, have the children do the following:

  Write two nouns.
  Write two verbs.
  Write two adjectives.
  Write a compound word.
  Write a word that means more than one.
  Write a word that shows possession.

  This can be a center activity completed by children working either with a partner or in a small group. It is also an excellent tool for assessment.

- On folded paper or flip books, write *sh, th, ch, and wh,* and draw a picture or write a word containing that sound.

  Choose vocabulary words from poems and stories. Write them under the appropriate digraph.
  Use letter families supplied by the group (or by you) and add sh, th, ch, and wh to make new words. Examples: *ick, thick, chick; in, chin, thin, shin; un, lunch, bunch, hunch, shun.*

Science

Two science projects are detailed here: winter birds and the use of a thermometer.

Winter birds

Step 1: Read information to the children about the cardinal and the blue jay.

Step 2: Write a cooperative experience story on chart paper, using facts learned from reading.

Step 3: Begin a bird notebook. As each bird is studied, the children are to write a factual report about it. A picture of the bird, drawn and colored as accurately as possible, should accompany each report. The pages are kept in a folder to be assembled into a book when the unit is completed.

Step 4: If possible, erect a bird feeder outside a classroom window where birds can be observed by the children. (Begin feeding the birds as early as possible because it takes time for them to be attracted to the feeder. At the school in which the authors teach, children are asked to bring sunflower seeds in September and the birds are fed throughout the school year. Thus when it is time for this unit, the birds have been coming to the feeder for many weeks.) Encourage the children to keep a class journal listing all birds they observe at the feeder. The journal should be kept in a convenient location near the window so that the children can make their entries easily. The species of birds observed each week can be graphed. At the end of the unit, a larger graph for the month can be completed by the class.

Use of a thermometer

- Ask the temperature at which water freezes.

- Ask the temperature at which snow falls.

- Ask the temperature at which snow melts.

- Teach children to read a Fahrenheit thermometer. Practice counting, by twos, the spaces between numbers.

- Record the temperature every day. Is it above freezing? Is it below freezing? How many degrees above or below freezing? This takes practice, but soon the children will become proficient at this mental math. Encourage them to share strategies for figuring out the differences in temperatures.

- Discuss the meaning of zero degrees and the concept of negative numbers when the temperature falls below this mark.

- Graph the monthly temperatures.

- Fill two large buckets with snow. Pack one tightly and the other loosely. Fill another bucket with ice. Put a thermometer in each bucket.

Determine which container melted first. Why?

Ask what was left in each container

Compare the temperature readings of each container.

Compare Fahrenheit and Celsius measurements.

Math

Materials

Large winter shape such as snowman, igloo, or snowflake

Enough cotton balls to cover the shape

Step 1: Hang a teacher-made snowman (about 36 by 40 inches) on the classroom door or on a bulletin board.

Step 2: Show the class a package of commercial cotton balls; give one to each child to examine. Ask each child to think about how many of these balls would be needed to cover the snowman. Discuss strategies for estimating. Ask each child to write an estimate on a small snowflake (cut earlier in the day) and to include his or her name.

Step 3: As the children complete their estimates, fasten the snowflakes around the snowman. Ask the children to come up and glue their cotton balls to the snowman. Let the class decide how many have been glued on so far. If no one immediately comes up with the answer, have them count by ones in unison while a child touches each person's head as they say a number. Begin a record on chart paper:

January 5. We added twenty cotton balls.

Step 4: The second day, give the children two cotton balls; the third day give them three, and so on. Attach them to the snowman. Each day record the number added.

Step 5: Let the class suggest ways to determine how many balls were added that day. This gives them practice in counting by 1, 2, 3, and 5. They also use various problem-solving techniques as they figure out the total for the day.

Step 6: When the snowman is full, ask the class how the total number of cotton balls can be determined. List all ideas on the board, and proceed with several. Perhaps someone will suggest adding all of the numbers together with calculators. Some children will be able to add the numbers mentally. It is helpful to others for these children to describe the process they followed after the problem has been solved.

Other children may figure out the number of tens in each number and add them together.

Step 7: After the total has been determined, have the children look at the estimates on the snowflakes to see whose estimate was closest to the actual number. Graph the number of children who exceeded the actual number and those who estimated lower numbers. Some may be able to figure out the differences between the actual number and their estimate.

Social Studies

Materials

Rosa Parks by Eloise Greenfield

Happy Birthday Martin Luther King by Jean Marzolo

Discuss Martin Luther King's role in the civil rights movement. Stress his belief in peaceful opposition and how it changed history for black Americans.

Discussion topics might be the following:

- Do you think it was right for black people to be required to sit in the back of the bus? Discuss the Atlanta bus boycott.

- Do you think Rosa Parks should have been put in jail for breaking the bus law? Do you think she should have been punished? Explain your answer.

- Do you think black people had the right to participate in peaceful marches? Why or why not?

Children can be encouraged to write stories about Martin Luther King, Jr. or write a cooperative chart story about facts they have learned.

Foreign Language

If possible, locate a person in the community who speaks Russian. Ask that person to visit the class and introduce some common words in the language. If no one is available for Russian, continue in the language used in other units and introduce the winter words: *snow, cold, snowflake, slide,* and *storm.*

Music

The study of "Dance of the Clowns" by Nikolai Rimsky-Korsakov (1844–1908) will be ongoing through the month of January. The Russian theme is familiar from the study of *The Nutcracker* in December, and it correlates with *The Mitten,* to be read later in the month.

Step 1: Rimsky-Korsakov lived in Russia. Discuss the Russian connection from the December unit, and help the children locate Russia on the map. Rimsky-Korsakov spent a major part of his life in Petrograd but was born in Tirhvin, Russia.

Step 2: Before listening to the music, tell the children the story of the Snow Maiden (Snegouratchka). This story comes from the ballet opera, *Snegouratchka* (Russian for "Snow Maiden"). The Snow Maiden is the daughter of King Frost. She has been brought up in the winter forest, safe from her father's enemy, the sun, whose rays would melt her lovely body. But one day Snegouratchka hears, from far away, the songs of a young shepherd. These cheery songs make her long to be a human instead of a chilly snow princess. She is so eager to be part of the real world that she goes to live with an old peasant couple who treat her as their own daughter. But in the end, Snegouratchka goes too near the sun and disappears beneath its shining rays.

In the last act of the opera, "Dance of the Clowns," the ancient legend ends sadly for the Snow Maiden but happily for the peasants. Joyfully they celebrate the coming of spring with a holiday. Like all Russian folk festivals, this one includes singing, dancing, and even a troop of tumblers and clowns to amuse the people.

Children should listen to this music over and over during the month. The music can be playing as they arrive in the morning, during snack time, during rest time, or at any opportunity for quiet listening. They should listen to the various instruments and try to identify a few. Don't stress the music excessively, but encourage listening for the enjoyment and fun heard in "Dance of the Clowns."

Art

- Adapting the collage technique of Ezra Jack Keats, the children can use various materials to make a cut- or torn-paper collage of snowy day fun. (No crayons or pencils are used for this activity.) Parts of *Snow Maiden* can be played while the children paint with water colors or tempera paint. Motivate them to paint freely, whatever the music suggests. This is also a good opportunity for finger painting.

- Children can construct creative stick or tube puppets of the clown, the Snow Maiden, Father Frost, and the Sun. Tongue depressors or 12-inch rulers work well for the sticks. Later the children can dramatize *Snegouratchka* with their stick puppets. This activity can be as elaborate or simple as time allows. The children can also make scenery as background for the dramatization.

Week 2: Overview

Instructional Books

Birds Are Animals by Judith Halloway and Clive Harper
Peter's Chair by Ezra Jack Keats
The Jacket I Wear in the Snow by Shirley Neitzel

Related Titles

Katy and the Big Snow by Virginia Lee Burton (to be read aloud)
Cross Country Cat by Mary Calhoun (to be read aloud)
A Winter Day by Douglas Florian (to be read aloud)
Happy Winter by Karen Gundersheimer (to be read aloud)
The Big Snow by Berta and Elmer Hader (to be read aloud)
Goggles by Ezra Jack Keats (to be read aloud)
Jennie's Hat by Ezra Jack Keats (to be read aloud)
Louie's Search by Ezra Jack Keats (to be read aloud)
The Trip by Ezra Jack Keats (to be read aloud)
Whistle for Willie by Ezra Jack Keats (to be read aloud)

Poems

"Snow" by Dorothy Aldis
"The Snowflake" by Walter de la Mare
"The More It Snows" by A. A. Milne
"White Snow, Bright Snow" by Alvin Tresselt

Objectives

1. **Phonetic skills**
   Review consonant digraphs previously introduced.
   Begin to understand r blends such as those in "hungry" and "bring."
   Review blends ou and ow.
   Introduce l blends.

Review long e, i, and a.

Review the function of y at the end of a word (*fly*) and when combined with a vowel (*play*).

2. **Structural analysis**

   Review and use nouns, verbs, and adjectives.

   Review the concept of compound words.

3. **Comprehension**

   Review the concepts of main idea and sequences.

   Introduce the concept of symbolism.

4. **Book reports**

Materials

Word cards in the shape of a jacket

Word cards in the shapes of snowballs and caps

Poetry and Skills Session

DAY 1

"White Snow, Bright Snow"

Step 1: Introduce the poem to the children. Read it aloud, inviting those who can to join in.

Step 2: Reread it aloud as a group, girls reading verse one, boys verse two, everyone verse three.

Step 3: Ask someone to state the main idea of the poem.

Step 4: Identify and circle adjectives by asking the children the following questions:

What word does the author use to describe the night? (*secret*)
Find some words that describe the snow. (*smooth, deep, white, bright, light*)
Find some adjectives that describe snowflakes. (*tiny, light*)

Step 5: Call attention to these circled adjectives frequently. Encourage the children to use them in their own speaking and writing.

DAY 2

"The More It Snows"

Step 1: Introduce "The More It Snows" by reading it aloud, asking those who can to join in.

Step 2: Tell the children that in the story, Winnie-the-Pooh makes up this poem. Allow time for discussion and for sharing the whimsy of the poem.

Step 3: Review digraphs previously taught by identifying them in the winter poetry.

Step 4: Teach the r consonant blends and again explain how consonant blends work.

DAY 3

"Snow"

Step 1: Review all poems and skills. Do this very quickly. Keep the pace moving and interesting. Note any skills that need to be retaught or reinforced, and include this in small group instruction.

Step 2: Introduce "Snow."

Step 3: After reading it together several times, discuss the symbolism. What does the author say about the fence posts (pointing out the compound phrase), the bushes, and the trees?

Step 4: Write the word "snow" on the board, or have someone frame it or point to it in the poem.

Step 5: Encourage the children to discuss what they learned about ow. Ask them to mark the words with the long o sound (*snow, snowy*).

Step 6: Ask the children to find a word with the other sound of ow (*gown*).

Step 7: Call attention to the word "snowy." Discuss the function of the y (it sounds like e), and review the fact that y becomes a vowel when it appears at the end of a word. Ask the children to try to find, or think of, some other words with y at the end but with the sound of the long e, long i, and long a.

Step 8: Make a chart list, or simply list the words on the board. Examples: baby, happy, lady, and ready. List words in which the y sounds like long i at the end of the word. Examples: *cry, try, my, dry,* and *fly*. List words in which it sounds like long a. Examples: *play, day, pray, away,* and *they*.

DAY 4

"The Snowflake"

Step 1: Introduce the poem. Read it to the children, inviting those who can to join in.

Step 2: Ask the children to identify words containing r blends. Examples: *filigree, great, crystals,* and *breathe.* Add these words to the ongoing chart list of r-blend words.

Step 3: Review digraphs. Examples: *white, vanish,* and *instantly.*

Step 4: Use the word "flakes" to introduce l blends.

Step 5: Point out that ow in "snow" spells the long o sound. Find some of the ow words in the other January poetry, and begin another ongoing list.

Step 6. Read the poem again. Distribute copies of the poem for your students to illustrate and include in their poetry notebooks.

DAY 5

Review January poetry and skills. Encourage the children to share their illustrations as they read their favorite poems today.

Reading Instruction

DAY 1

The Jacket I Wear in the Snow

Shared Reading

Step 1: Introduce *The Jacket I Wear in the Snow.*

Step 2: Ask a volunteer to find the author's and illustrator's names. Discuss what each contributed to the book.

Step 3: Ask the children to predict what this book will be about, based on the title and cover art. Record their predictions.

Step 4: Read the book aloud to the class, calling their attention to the rebus art and explaining that the pictures are substitutes for words. Show them that a picture for the word "zipper" appears on one left-hand page and that they will see the zipper again on the right-hand page in picture form.

Step 5: Reread the book together.

Step 6: Read one of the Ezra Jack Keats selections aloud to the class. Review Keats' settings, characters, and illustrations.

Note: Before beginning this unit, assemble as many Keats titles as possible (duplicates are a plus). Arrange them in a separate Keats reading center readily accessible to the children.

Small Group Instruction

Step 1: Mix ability levels and rercad *The Jacket I Wear in the Snow*.

Step 2: Ask the children to recall the order of the various articles of clothing in the book. List their suggestions on the board, and then compare their list with the sequence in the book. Point out that the order is reversed when the mother removes the articles of clothing.

Step 3: Challenge the students to recall the reverse order, list it on the board, and then have them check their accuracy with the book.

Step 4: Have the children go back quickly through parts of the book to identify words containing the th and ch digraphs. There are many ch words.

DAY 2

The Jacket I Wear in the Snow

Shared Reading

Using the big book, recap the story with the children. Discuss as follows:

- Did you like the story? Why or why not?

- Tell your favorite part or illustration. Why did you like this part or illustration best?

- How do you feel about the ending?

- Does this story remind you of something that has happened to you?

Small Group Instruction

Divide the children into small groups for direct instruction, according to the needs of individuals.

EL: Using word cards with the target vocabulary, play games with this group. The children may choose a word, read it, and use it in a sentence. They can look for a word that holds a jacket together: "zipper"; something that keeps your hands warm: "mittens." One child can choose a word, find a sentence in the book that contains the word, and read the sentence to the group.

TL: Reread *The Jacket . . .* with the children to determine their level of mastery. If they are ready, move on to the next book. However, if the majority of this group is still struggling with the vocabulary, use some of the activities of the previous group.

AL: Introduce *Peter's Chair*. Plan to complete the reading of the book at the close of the small-group session the next day. Less mature readers can also appreciate and benefit from reading this book. The illustrations give excellent context clues, and the text is relatively easy.

The main objective for this selection is comprehension. Read this book aloud in unison. The children can then take turns reading, or it can be read silently, depending on the ability of the group. Supply the words immediately if a child needs support.

DAY 3

Shared Reading

Step 1: Before this session, prepare some word cards for vocabulary work. Write the targeted words on cards cut in the shape of a jacket.

Step 2: Print some text from the book on chart paper (using the words written on the cards), omitting words that will be supplied by the children. Example:

This is the _____ all itchy and warm, (sweater)
that meets the _____ that hang from each arm. (mittens)

Step 2: Spend some time identifying r blends in the big book. Do the same with digraphs. Not only does this activity help the reader recognize the sound of the blends, it also reinforces story vocabulary and decoding skills.

Small Group Instruction

EL: If it is appropriate for a group of children to continue working with *The Jacket . . .* , the following activities can be completed over the next two sessions.

- Play vocabulary games with the word cards. If magnetic tape has been attached to the backs of the cards, they will stick to the chalkboards and can be used in the following ways:

Draw on the board the articles of clothing that the child wore. Have the students match a word card to the article. Arrange the words naming articles of clothing in the sequence in which they appeared in the book. Reverse the order.

Draw two large jackets on the board. Write the heading *How clothes can feel* over one and *Words that tell where* over the other. Display word cards: *under, on, hot, jacket, itchy, sweater, over, stiff,* and *warm.* Allow the children to take turns placing a word on a correct jacket.

This activity can be varied by changing the headings on the jackets to *nouns, verbs, short vowels,* or *long vowels.* Words can also be placed on one jacket and the children asked to suggest a synonym or an antonym to be written on the second jacket.

- Comprehension discussion questions can include the following:

Has the zipper on your jacket ever gotten stuck or broken? Why is that a problem?
Do you have any clothes that are itchy? Do enjoy wearing them?
Tell about a time you have gone sledding. Did you have any problems, or was it all great fun?

TL and AL: Complete guided reading of *Peter's Chair*. Ask the following questions of both groups. It is appropriate to expect more of the more skilled readers. Those who are gaining confidence may not see some of the subtleties that more mature children grasp. Encourage all children to use complete sentences and expand brief answers.

- What was the main problem in the book? This will present an excellent opportunity for some children to "safely" discuss negative feelings when there is a new baby brother or sister. What did his parents do that made Peter feel angry? Children may read parts of the text that answer this question. Have your parents ever done anything like that? How did you feel about it?

- What did he do with his chair? Why?

- How did Peter plan to solve the problem? Do you think his idea was a good one? Why or why not?

- What did Peter take when he decided to run away from home? Who is the baby in the picture outside Peter's house? What would you take if you were going to run away?

- How did Peter solve the problem? How did he tease his mother?

- Did Peter's parents love him? How could you tell?

- Why did Peter decide to give his chair to his baby sister, Susie?

DAY 4

Shared Reading

Step 1: From the big book of *The Jacket* . . . , have the children identify rhyming words. Write them on the board and then add another word or words to the ones listed. Write these pairs on cards shaped like a snowball and a cap.

Step 2: Have the students take turns matching the words. This game can be played by everyone during shared reading and then placed in a center for later play, either individually or with a partner.

Small Group Instruction

Book Reports

Display all of the Keats books you have gathered. It is helpful to have two of each title so the children can work in pairs; however, two children can share one book. Suggest that the class divide itself into sets of two. It is appropriate for you to direct this process so that children are paired for successful conclusion of this assignment.

Ask each set of partners to choose a book to read together. The children will read the book either independently or with a partner. Tell them that they are to make a report to their group or to the class as a whole, depending upon size and time. They will also be responsible for individual book projects, which you will suggest. Each set of partners may choose the one they want to do. As soon as the books are chosen, the children should be encouraged to find a quiet spot and begin reading. Reports should include the following:

> Title and author
> Main characters
> Setting
> Problem (The children should not tell how the problem was solved because that will spoil the story for others who may want to read the book.)
> Why the child liked or disliked the book
> Why the child would or would not recommend the book to a friend

For the children in the class who can't handle this assignment, it is appropriate to continue with the suggested activities from day 3. Other alternatives might be to read *Louie's Search, Whistle for Willie, Goggles,* or *The Trip.*

DAY 5

Shared Reading

Step 1: Continue the activities of the previous session. You can continue conferences with the pairs of children reading the individual Keats books. Discuss their book, give them help where needed, and listen to them read favorite parts of the story.

Step 2: Set a time for them to share their book orally with the group. Have each set of partners choose a book project from the following suggestions:

Literature report
Keats-inspired collage (based on the story the child is reading) with a brief story report recapping the story line
Diorama or triorama based on the story, with a brief report.

Independent Activities

Materials

12-by-18-inch newsprint

12-by-18-inch drawing paper

Pattern of a child's body for paper doll project

Yarn for hair

Construction paper for clothing

Tongue depressors

Large plastic cups

Pictures of objects (which may be cut from a catalog or old workbook), glued to heavy paper and laminated

Extension Activities

- Prepare literature reports based on instructional books.

- Using a piece of 12-by-18-inch paper, draw an outline of a child so that it resembles the body of a paper doll. Instruct children to glue on yarn hair or hair made from cut and curled paper and to add the other features. They can then draw, decorate, and cut out several sets of winter clothing for the figure. Some of the outfits might be a warm-up suit, a ski or ice-skating outfit, or a jacket to wear in the snow. The clothing should have tabs for attaching to the figure. Some children can make an extra outfit to place in a classroom store. (See the math activities.)

- Write lists of nouns, verbs, and adjectives from the reading or poetry books.

- Fold 12-by-18-inch paper in fourths. Write one of the blends from the week in each box. Illustrate them. Some children should be encouraged to write the words.

- Provide the children with circles cut from paper. Fold in fourths. Make a blend wheel with the same activities described above. Attach a tongue depressor for a handle.

- Rewrite a Keats story or write a new ending to one.

- Encourage children to write a creative winter poem or short rhyming story.

- Write a story using rebus pictures.

Small Group and Center Activities

- Have vocabulary words from *The Jacket I Wear in the Snow* available at the center whenever they are not in use for instruction.

  Sort the words into nouns, verbs, and adjectives (a "clue" could be placed on the back).
  Arrange the words in alphabetical order.
  Sort the words according to long and short vowel sounds.

- Have rhyming words matching game from day 4, Shared Reading, available in a center.

- Label large plastic cups with blends that you have taught. Cut pictures from an old workbook or magazine, and have the children sort the correct blend word into the proper blend cup. If you laminate the whole workbook page before cutting the pictures apart, they will last longer. Any phonics book will have many pictures appropriate for this purpose.

Science

- Continue the thermometer and temperature activities from week 1.

- After completing the experiments with snow and ice, pose these scientific questions:

  Which melts faster, snow or ice? Why?
  Which evaporates first, cold water or hot water? Why?
  How are water, snow, and ice related?
  Perhaps some of the children can find sources in the library to prove their answers.

- Continue the unit on birds. Read information to the children about the black-capped chickadee and the red-headed woodpecker. Encourage the children to find material on their own to share with the class.

- Write a class experience story on chart paper from information learned about each of these birds.

- Have the children write their own factual reports, which they illustrate, to be included in their bird notebooks.

- Assemble a center of as many appropriate bird books as possible for the children to read during free time. This is an excellent way to help them learn to find information on their own.

- Encourage the children to keep the class bird-watching journal up-to-date. Continue graphing activities on the birds observed, favorite birds, or other categories suggested by the children.

- Ask each child to bring a pine cone to school. Have the children coat the pine cones with peanut butter and then roll them in fine mixed bird seed. They then lay the pine cones in the bushes near the classroom windows so they can watch the birds enjoying their treats.

- Read *Birds Are Animals* in small groups. Bring the children together for the discussion questions in the back of the book.

Math

- Continue the snowman estimating activity begun during week 1.

- Instruct the children to trace their hands to make a pair of mittens. Decorate the mittens and fasten them together with a length of yarn. Hang these pairs around the room or on a clothesline to reinforce counting by twos.

- Discuss pairs. Ask the children to identify the articles of clothing in *The Jacket* . . . that come in pairs. Ask them to suggest examples of pairs they can see in the classroom: eyes, legs, pigtails or braids, gym shoes, and so on.

- Arrange the extra outfits made for the figures of children into a class clothing store. Give the children some play money to purchase clothing for their dolls. Have the more able children take turns acting as the cashier. Encourage them to plan what they want to buy and budget their money. This could be an ongoing, growing project with children continuing to design new and different outfits. Some children might enjoy placing orders for specific outfits in certain colors. Children can figure out ways to earn their play money to purchase more clothing. Some of the children may enjoy planning and staging a fashion show.

Foreign Language

Continue introducing various winter words in the target language. Words associated with birds are also appropriate: seeds, names of birds, song, colors, and parts of a bird, such as wing, feet, beak, and eye.

Music

Continue playing and discussing "Dance of the Clowns" and "Dance of the Tumblers" by Rimsky-Korsakov. The children can be working on the stick puppets in a center to coordinate with this music. Encourage movement with the music when appropriate.

Art

Materials

Wallpaper books

Construction paper

- The entire class might enjoy making cut- and torn-paper collages inspired by Keats. Provide students with old wallpaper sample books, magazines, and lots of paper scraps. Encourage them to mix materials (paint, wallpaper, and colored paper) to create interesting pictures.

- Read *Jennie's Hat* to the class. Make the children aware of the wonderful pictures. The girls in the class will especially enjoy creating collages based on this book. The boys might be inspired to make baseball-style hats. Motivate the children to design fantastic hats for their school store. They may also enjoy designing fantastic big hats, using different materials. Show them how to construct basic three-dimensional flowers, and then let their imaginations and creativity take over. Display their hats on the bulletin board or on a clothesline in the room.

Week 3: Overview

Instructional Books

The Mitten by Jan Brett
The Mitten by Alvin Tresselt

Related Titles

Annie and the Wild Animals by Jan Brett (to be read aloud)
The Mystery of the Old Red Mitten by Steven Kellogg (to be read aloud)
A New Coat for Anna by Harriet Ziefert (to be read aloud)

Poems

The Mitten Song by Marie Louise Allen
Icy by Rhonda Bachmeister
The Mitten Poem by Eleanor Ripp

Objectives

1. **Phonetic skills**
   Begin to understand initial, medial, and final th.
   Add endings to words with a final e.
2. **Structural skills**
   Begin to understand synonyms.
   Begin to understand homonyms.
3. **Comprehension**
   Continue to make predictions.

Materials

Cards with the names of the animals from "The Mitten Poem"

Cards with ordinal numbers corresponding to the animals

Word cards in the shape of a mitten

Construction paper in light colors

Mitten pattern

Large mitten made of paper and stapled or sewn together

Poetry and Skills Session

DAY 1

"The Mitten Song"

Step 1: Introduce "The Mitten Song." Many of the children will be familiar with it, so begin right away to sing the poem. The children can perform the finger motions as they sing.

Step 2: Call attention to the mittens displayed around the room. Count them by twos.

Step 3: Identify all of the th words. Mark them with a washable pen. Compare the sound of th in *thumb* with that in *together, weather,* and *whether*.

Step 4: Discuss *weather* and *whether*. Guide the children in verbalizing that these words sound the same but are spelled differently and have different meanings. Introduce the term *homonym*, but don't expect the children to master the meaning at this time. Ask the children to think of other words that sound the same but mean different things. Examples: *meat - meet, write - right*.

DAY 2

Icy

Step 1: Display the poem *Icy*. Ask a volunteer to read the title.

Step 2: Ask the children to look at the poem to see how many words they know. Call on individuals to point to a word, read it, and circle the word with a washable pen. Continue until all words have been circled. The children may be surprised to find that they know almost all of the words.

Step 3: Read the poem aloud as a group. This strategy works well because all have the opportunity to contribute. When all are reading together, it is not obvious when someone does not know a word.

Step 4: Discuss the role of the y as a vowel in the words *icy, slippery,* and *tummy*.

Step 5: Review the l blends.

Step 6: Compare the long and short i in *slip* and *slide*. Review the rule of the final e. Ask the students to find other short i words and circle them with a washable pen.

Step 7: Review the capitalization of I.

DAY 3

Review the January poetry and skills.

DAY 4

The Mitten Poem

Step 1: Most of the children will be able to read this poem independently. Ask them to read it silently, and then ask the following questions:

Which animals are mentioned in the poem?
What did the poem tell about the animals?

They should recognize that the animals are the same as those in Brett's *The Mitten* and entered the mitten in the same sequence.

Step 2: Invite volunteers either to frame the animal names with their hands or to circle the word with a washable pen.

Step 3: Write the names of the animals on one set of cards and corresponding ordinal numbers on another. Ask the children to match them. Example: "first - mole."

Step 4: When all cards are matched, ask questions such as the following:
Which animal was third?
What is the number word that tells when the fox arrived?

This is an appropriate center activity after it has been used with the whole group.

Step 5: Review verbs by having individuals frame or circle words that tell what the animals did.

DAY 5

Children are to bring poetry notebooks to the group and read their favorite poems as a solo, duet, trio, or quartet. It is their choice.

Reading Instruction

DAY 1

The Mitten **by Jan Brett**

Shared Reading

Step 1: Display the big book *The Mitten* by Jan Brett.

Step 2: Ask the students to imagine being in a forest during a snowstorm. What animals and trees did they see? What animals live in the forest that they may not have seen?

Step 3: Ask them how these woodland animals keep warm during the cold winter? Briefly discuss warm-blooded animals and how they stay warm: thick fur; heavy, oily feathers; and hibernation.

Step 4: Ask someone to name the animals on the front of the book and suggest ways for them to stay warm.

Step 5: Request predictions about the content of the book. Record the predictions for later use.

Step 6: Read the author's name to the children and tell them what "adapted" means. Read the brief biography of Jan Brett.

Biographical Sketch of Jan Brett

Jan Brett knew in kindergarten that she would be an illustrator of children's books. She was shy around other children and was much happier to be alone with her pencils, crayons, and paper. She always felt frustrated because the illustrations in her childhood books did not have enough detail, so she has corrected that problem in her own drawings.

Jan Brett lives in Massachusetts and spends summers in the mountains, where the scenery and animals stimulate her artistic imagination. She likes to use real animals and people to model for her stories. She says that she uses borders when she can't get all of her ideas into her pictures. (Kovacs and Preller 1993)

Small Group Instruction

Note: When planning this week's reading group instruction, set aside one day to hear the Ezra Jack Keats oral reports and to let the children choose another Keats book. Plan regular conferences with the children who are doing Keats book projects, offering encouragement and assistance.

Step 1: Bring the children together in mixed ability groups to read *The Mitten* orally and to respond to the story.

Step 2: Encourage students to identify the words that are new and to define those that they do not understand. *Lumbered* and *silhouetted* will probably be new to some.

Step 3: Discuss the unfamiliar animals such as hedgehog and badger.

DAY 2

The Mitten by Jan Brett

Shared Reading

Step 1: Review *The Mitten*. Read it together or by taking turns in small groups of two, three, or four. (These can be referred to as *duets, trios,* and *quartets*. The children soon learn the numbers that form such groups.)

Step 2: Ask the children to describe what is happening in each picture. Encourage them to give specific details about the appearance of each animal. Example: "The bear is huge, and it has brown fur, a long snout, and sharp claws."

Step 3: Have the children reread the book. Ask them how they know which animal will come next in the story.

Small Group Instruction

EL: This should be a brief review and drill of words from the previous session.

Step 1: Select a variety of words.

Step 2: Ask a volunteer to read a word and then use it in a sentence.

Step 3: Write these sentences on the board and then use them for the reading instruction. Continue adding a few words each day to the vocabulary list.

TL:

Step 1: Discuss the beautiful Ukrainian folk art in Baba's sitting room. Explain to the children that Ukrainian people also have a special technique for decorating Easter eggs. Perhaps someone can bring some of these eggs to school to show the class.

Step 2: As the story is read, ask the children to find words that describe how the animals look and read that passage aloud.

Step 3: Ask the children to begin making a list of words they would like to learn. They can record these on writing paper or on cards cut in the shape of a mitten. The list of words may vary according to the reading level of each child. You should offer suggestions about the choice of words. Continue adding to this vocabulary list during the week.

AL: Distribute writing paper to the children. Have them fold it into thirds. Label each section *noun, verb,* or *adjective.* As they read the book silently, they should write at least three words in each category.

DAY 3

The Mitten by Alvin Tresselt

Shared Reading

Step 1: Read *The Mitten* by Alvin Tresselt to the class, taking time to let them look carefully at the pictures.

Step 2: Reread parts of the Jan Brett edition. Ask the children to compare the two. Use a Venn diagram for this comparison.

Step 3: Draw the diagram as large as possible on the chalkboard, or have one pre-prepared on poster board. The poster board can be laminated for repeated use. This is a good opportunity for the evaluation of comprehension as the children compare and contrast the content of the two versions. You can make a formal assessment by asking the children to do this as a paper-and-pencil activity.

Step 4: Upon completion of the diagram, discuss the material that has been recorded:

Were the books more alike or different?
What were some differences?
What was the same?
Which version did individuals like best? Why? Be specific!

Small Group Instruction

Step 1: Before these sessions begin, cut some construction paper into the shape of mittens and write some of the vocabulary words on them. Store the small mittens in a larger mitten made out of sturdy paper and sewn together to resemble the one in the story.
Step 2: Continue adding to the vocabulary list.
Step 3: Reread the book with the children. Ask them to look for words that tell how each animal moves. Read the passages orally.

DAY 4

The Mitten by Jan Brett

Shared Reading

Step 1: Briefly review the story. Pass out the vocabulary cards. As the story is read, each word is held up as it appears in the story.
Step 2: Ask the children to identify the passages that describe how each animal moved. Make a list of the words on the board. Have volunteers come up to underline the root word with red chalk and circle the ending with blue chalk.

Small Group Instruction

For this session, group the children according to mastery of root words. Use the following activities:

EL: Write a list of simple words that have regular endings. Examples: *runs, watching,* and *planted.* Use this time to assess, reteach, and reinforce this skill.

TL: Contrast words that are unchanged when the ending is added to some in which an e has been dropped. Examples: *hiding, coming.* Use this time to assess and reteach as needed.

AL:

Step 1: Write a list of root words on the board. Have the children add endings. These words should include some that are unchanged and some ending in e.

Step 2: Introduce the rule that when a word ends in a consonant preceded by a vowel, the consonant must be doubled before adding the ending. Examples: *set - setting, cut - cutting.* Assess the level of mastery in this group. Regroup at a later time for those who still need reinforcement.

DAY 5

***The Mitten* by Jan Brett**

Shared Reading

Step 1: Read *The Mitten* for pure enjoyment.
Step 2: Initiate a book talk with questions such as the following:

How are Niki's clothes different?
How is his grandmother's house different? Why?
How might Niki have felt when he realized his mitten was lost?
What did Baba mean when she said, "When you come home, first I will look to see if you are safe and sound, but then I will look to see if you still have your mittens."
What is Niki doing while the animals are in his mitten? Does he see the animals?
What do you think Baba is saying to Niki on the very last page?
How could this folk tale have ended differently?

Small Group Instruction

Encourage all children to read the book with a friend at some time during the day.

EL:

Step 1: Write sentences on the board, omitting words.
Step 2: Ask individuals in the group to supply the missing words and read the sentences.
Step 3: Match animal names with the correct pictures in the book.

TL: Initiate a vocabulary game by asking the children to bring their vocabulary lists to the group. By either using their lists or pulling a word card from the large mitten, ask a volunteer in the group to define the word by using it in a sentence. This game can be varied by asking another child to name a word with a particular vowel sound, a word with an ending, an animal's name, or a contraction. One child can give a definition and another can find the word.

AL: Make arrangements with the school librarian for this group to research the following in the library:

> Other Jan Brett books
> Where Niki lived and what can be learned about his country
> Whether badgers live near your school
> Information about moles and other animals in the book

Allow the children to work as partners or in small groups.

Independent Activities

Materials

Mitten-shaped books for student writing

Two large mittens cut from tag board with holes punched around edges

Yarn for sewing mitten together

Small cards with pictures of animals

Small cards with corresponding names of animals

Materials for making silhouettes of students: white paper and an oversized flashlight

Pairs of mittens cut from construction paper

Extension Activities

- Have the students write their versions of *The Mitten,* using mitten-shaped books. The story might be written from the perspective of one of the animals. Suppose one of the animals lost something and Niki found it. What might happen?

- Have the children pretend they are with MucLuc, an Inuit child in Alaska. MucLuc has lost his mitten (or his bag). Ask the children to write a new folk tale. Which animals would move in? What color would his mitten (or bag) be? What would it be made of? What could cause the animals to scatter? This activity can be adapted to a child in a tropical area such as the rain forest. Make a class big book with the children's original folk tales and illustrations.

- Cut out two large mittens from tag board or other heavy paper. The students can do this using a pattern; both pieces must be the same shape and size. Help them punch holes evenly around both mittens.

Then, with large needles and yarn, sew the pieces together, leaving an opening at the cuff. Decorate the mitten with a design inspired by the illustrations in the book. For young children, the yarn can be fastened to a small safety pin, which can be used to weave the yarn in and out of the holes. The vocabulary words are copied on small cards and stored in the mitten. Pictures of the animals can be drawn on small cards and their names printed on additional cards. These are placed in the mitten in correct story sequence and/or used as a matching game.

- A reproducible adaptation of *The Mitten,* illustrated by Jo Anna Paehlmann, is available. (Copycat Press Inc., 1991.) This may be helpful for use with less mature readers.

- To reinforce the word "silhouette," make a silhouette of each child in the class. Tape white paper to the chalkboard or a free wall. Have a child stand in profile in front of the paper. Darken the room and shine an oversized flashlight at the child. The silhouette will appear on the paper. Trace the shape and cut it out. Mount the white silhouette on black paper.

- Use grids for the following activity, providing one for each child. Help the children determine the questions to be asked and how they will record the responses.

  Comparison grid (see p. 70): compare characters, evaluating each character as good, bad, kind, or unkind.
  Compare the animals in the same way.
  Compare various versions of *The Mitten.*
  Compare *The Mitten* with other Jan Brett stories.

Small Group and Center Activities

- Put the vocabulary cards in the large mitten you made (mentioned in the discussion for small group instruction on day 3). Place the mitten in a center so the children can play games with the words.

- Make pairs of mittens from construction paper. Place them in a large mitten or cardboard copy of Baba's house. Write words on the mittens. Have the children do the following:

  Match opposites
  Match synonyms and homonyms
  Make compound words
  Identify specific long and short vowel sounds in words
  Find root words and match appropriate endings

Name _____

Comparison Grid	Story 1	Story 2
Title		
Setting		
Main Characters		
Problem		
Attempts to solve the problem		
How the problem was solved		
How characters felt at the end		

Month by Month © 1995 Zephyr Press, Tucson, AZ

- Make blank tapes available for the children, allowing them to take turns reading and recording a favorite page or passage from *The Mitten*. Keep these in the listening center for others to hear.

Science

- Research the animals in both books. Various topics for discussion might be as follows:

  How do the mole and hedgehog protect themselves?
  How, or why, is it helpful for an animal to be the same color as its environment? Example: Why is the snowshoe rabbit white?

- After this information has been discussed, help the children make one or more class charts on the following topics: Name of the animal and how it protects itself, name of the animal and what it eats, name of the animal and where it lives.

- After reading the book and completing additional research on the animals, encourage the children to write riddles about an animal. Direct them to write four clues about each animal, such as how it looks, what it eats, where it lives, and some habit or a sound it makes. Later these riddles can be copied (editing the mistakes) on large index cards and placed in a box in the science center. Each child is to choose a riddle, write the name of the animal, and illustrate it. These can then be bound together into a class book. After the book is completed, the children match the riddles with the pictures. This can be an ongoing reading and partner activity.

Math

- Have the children trace around their hands to make a pair of mittens. Decorate and cut them out, and then fasten them together with a length of yarn. Tape these pairs of mittens along the chalkboard, on a line stretched across the room, or on the walls around the room.

- Teach or reinforce the concept of counting by twos. Let the children take turns using a pointer to lead the class in counting.

- Discuss and make a list of other things that come in pairs. Have pairs of children stand around the room and count by twos.

- Have volunteers arrange pictures and names of animals in the sequence in which they appeared in the story. Other children can match ordinal number words, "first" through "eighth," beside the animal's name. Ask the following questions:

Which animal is fourth?
In what place did the owl enter the mitten?
If the rabbit is second, how many animals come after it?
If the bear is seventh, how many come before it?
Which animal is first? Last? Use Niki and Baba to reinforce "first" through "tenth."

- Ask each child to find an old mitten at home and fill it with as many small objects as can be squeezed into it. Bring it to school to share with the class. Ask and discuss the following math questions:

Who was able to get the most objects in the mitten? Why?
Who had the least? Why?
Why was one child able to get more in than another?
Discuss the size of the mittens.
Discuss expansion and what the mittens are made of. Would one stretch more than another?
Have the children pick a partner and compare their mittens.
Make math sentences: *If John has 6 objects and Jane has 4, who has the most, or least? Write number sentences.*
Sort the objects by category. The students have to decide how to categorize the objects.
Arrange the objects into sets for addition and subtraction.

- Have the children decide how many animals were in the mitten after the owl moved in. Ask how many animals there would be if three skunks moved in. Solve the problem with counters; then have the children write the number sentence on their slates. After modeling a few of these number stories using both addition and subtraction, encourage volunteers to tell their own stories for the class to solve.

Social Studies

Step 1: Assist the children in finding Ukraine on a world map. Insert a push pin into that place.

Step 2: Have them identify their part of the United States and insert a push pin there. Help the children generalize that Ukraine is very far away.

Step 3: Presumably the class has discussed folk tales, so the students will understand the concept. Ask how they think a story from a place so far away might have gotten to their home town.

Step 4: Read other folk tales or make them available.

Step 5: Research Ukraine together. Discuss its customs, food, art, climate, and so on. With the help of the school librarian, have the children who are able go to the library to research this country. If possible, have materials available in the classroom as well.

Step 6: Encourage the children to write a simple report on one of the areas of research.

Step 7: Invite someone who has lived in Ukraine or visited the country to speak to the class, sharing information, pictures, objects of art, and perhaps some samples of food.

Foreign Language

Locate someone to teach the children a Ukrainian folk song. Seek help at a nearby high school or college and teach the children some words in Russian. Example: "Baba" means "grandmother."

Music

- Continue the activities suggested for the previous week in conjunction with the music of Rimsky-Korsakov's *Snow Maiden*.

- Sing "Mitten Song," complete with hand movements. Marching, snapping fingers, and clapping in time with the music are also fun for the children and a good way to get "the wiggles" out!

Art

Step 1: Display from the story the picture that illustrates Ukrainian art on the clothes, the dishes, and the fireplace. Observe the borders of the pages throughout the book.

Step 2: Give each child a paper plate. Ask them all to draw a design in the center. They should then fold the plate into four equal sections and repeat a design in each. Encourage the use of the same colors and patterns. Display the Ukrainian plates in the room.

Step 3: Suggest the use of the Ukrainian border on mitten-shaped stories or other papers.

Week 4: Overview

Instructional Books

Feathers for Lunch by Lois Ehlert
Birds Are Animals by Judith Halloway and Clive Harper
Tacky the Penguin by Helen Lester

Related Titles

Harriet and Walt by Nancy Carlson (to be read aloud)
Goodbye Geese by Nancy White Carlstrom (to be read aloud)
Antarctica by Helen Cowcher (to be read aloud)
Birds at Home by Marguerite Henry (to be read aloud)
The Bird Feeder Book by Donald and Lillian Stokes (to be read aloud)
A Year of Birds by Ashley Wolff (to be read aloud)
Little Penguin's Tale by Audrey Wood (to be read aloud)
Owl Moon by Jane Yolen (to be read aloud)

Poems

"Chickadee" by Hilda Conkling
"Crumbs" by Walter de la Mare
"The Snow Bird" by Frank Dempster Sherman
"The Penguin" by Rozanne Williams

Objectives

1. **Phonetic skills**
   Begin to understand the digraph ck.
   Review digraphs previously introduced.
   Reinforce oo.
   Begin to understand the soft sound of g.
2. **Structural skills**
   Begin to understand antonyms.
   Review possessive nouns.
   Review apostrophes.
3. **Comprehension**
   Review the concepts of fact and fiction.

Materials

Word cards in the shape of penguins

Poetry and Skills Session

DAY 1

"The Snow Bird"

Step 1: Review the poem with the class. Read it as a group.

Step 2: Read the poem again, reinforcing comprehension.

Step 3: Ask the following questions:

Is the snow bird any special kind? Name some birds that could be called "snow birds."
What is the meaning of the word "delight"? Provide a synonym for it.
Why was the bird delighted to find the crumbs?
Why is it important to feed birds in the winter?
How could the snow be printed with stars?

Step 4: Point to words in the poem and ask for antonyms. Example: white - black.

Step 5: Reinforce other phonetic strategies as needed.

DAY 2

"Crumbs"

Step 1: Reread "The Snow Bird" and briefly review the previous session.

Step 2: Introduce "Crumbs" and read it to the class. Ask about the main idea. To whom did the "I" refer? Why is it a capital letter?

Step 3: Request volunteers to identify words or phrases that describe winter. This reinforces vocabulary development.

Step 4: Focus on "worm's." Write it on the board and ask what the apostrophe means. Explain that it means that something belongs to the worm. Compare the plural of "worm" to the possessive. Give other examples of possessives, using children in the class.

Step 5: Look through other poems to identify possessive forms.

DAY 3

"The Penguin"

Step 1: Introduce "The Penguin."

Step 2: Display pictures of penguins.

Step 3: Read "The Penguin." If time permits, read *Little Penguin's Tale*.

Step 4: Return to the poem and read it aloud as a group.

Step 5: Discuss how the penguin is different from other birds. Encourage the children to tell what they know about these birds, using information from the books just read. Put these facts on a chart.

DAY 4

"Chickadee"

This poem contains a great amount of symbolism, so it may be appropriate to read the poem to the children and then ask them to interpret it. The beauty lies in the opportunity for different interpretations. Encourage children to share their ideas. There are no wrong answers.

Step 1: Ask what time of year it is. How do you know? Based on the study of the chickadee, why is it in an apple tree?

Step 2: Reinforce the consonant digraph ck in *chickadee*. Compare this word with some that have this blend at the end. Examples: *chick* and *rack*.

Step 3: Review other consonant blends: sl, sm, br, and dr.

Step 4: Review the long e in *see, tree, me, sleepy,* and *sea*. Compare with words that contain a short e.

Step 5: Discuss the oo in *smooth*. Why doesn't oo spell the long o sound? Find similar examples in other poems.

Step 6: Discuss the soft g in *gently*. Reinforce the fact that g followed by e, i, or y sounds like a j. Find similar examples in other text.

DAY 5

Today is free-choice day. The children can choose favorite poems to read alone or with a friend.

Reading Instruction

DAY 1

Birds Are Animals

Shared Reading

Step 1: Ideally each child should have a copy of this book or should share it with no more than one other child. Give the class time to look through the book.

Step 2: Read the book together, using directed reading strategies. Supply unknown words immediately. If copies of the book are limited, it can be read in small groups.

Small Group Instruction

Bring the children together in mixed ability groups to read *Birds Are Animals* orally. Stop after each page to discuss the material and to identify the birds. Encourage the children to identify words that are new to them. Write these words on vocabulary cards, and use them for reinforcement.

DAY 2

Shared Reading

Begin this session with a review of the facts in *Birds Are Animals*. Conduct a general discussion about birds, drawing information from children who know a lot about birds.

Devote the remainder of the session to the presentation of new material on birds. Factual books on this subject are available through community and school libraries. These books are written on a variety of levels. They have excellent pictures and can be read either to the class or individually by the more independent readers. Place a selection of these in an accessible location so that children who want to know more about this subject can read during their free time. This is another way to provide in-depth content to children who are ready for more than the curriculum offers.

Small Group Instruction

EL:
Step 1: Review the targeted vocabulary. Briefly discuss decoding skills that apply to these words.
Step 2: Reread *Birds are Animals* orally.
Step 3: If time allows, ask individuals to read the questions at the end of the story while others find the answers in the text.

TL:
Step 1: Discuss the content of the book.
Step 2: Review words that are new or troublesome. Then read the book silently.
Step 3: Ask volunteers to read the questions at the end of the book. Direct the children to locate the material that answers the questions.
Step 4: Encourage them to make up some questions of their own and have others find the answers in the book.

AL:
Step 1: Identify the birds pictured in the book.
Step 2: Begin a list of birds that are commonly seen in the winter.

Step 3: Gather material about these birds. What do they eat? How do they protect themselves in very cold weather? What can people do to help them during the harsh winter months?

DAY 3

Tacky the Penguin

Shared Reading

Step 1: Discuss the information about penguins presented during the poetry session.

Step 2: Ask the class what they know about penguins. Write these responses on chart paper.

Step 3: Encourage the children to ask questions about penguins. Record these questions on a chart entitled, "What we'd like to know about penguins."

Step 4: Introduce *Tacky the Penguin*. Follow the usual procedure for predicting the content of the story. At this time, do not read the book to the class but tell them they will find out about the story during small group time.

Small Group Instruction

EL:

Step 1: Follow directed reading strategies with this group, moving slowly and offering support as needed.

Step 2: Evaluate the predictions.

Step 3: Have the students decide which words from the text they would like to target for vocabulary work.

Step 4: Record the story on a tape. Have this group listen to the story, following the text as it is read.

TL:

Step 1: Ask whether the children think this book is fact or fiction. Why? What will be the setting of the book? Who will be the main character?

Step 2: Have the children silently read one or two pages at a time. Immediately supply any words that are difficult, making a note of them. At the end of the session, put these words on the board and discuss decoding strategies.

Step 3: Discuss the story. Was it fact or fiction? Support the answer.

AL:

Step 1: Read the book silently. Compare it to the predictions. Which were on target? Do any of the predictions suggest a new story?

Step 2: Look at a world map and locate Tacky's home. What is their opinion of Tacky? Do they have any friends like Tacky? Are they like him? Explain the answers.

Step 3: Ask whether it bothered Tacky to be different. Students must support their answers. Ask the children to tell of an experience in which they felt different from the group.

DAY 4

Tacky the Penguin

Shared Reading

Step 1: Conduct a general discussion about *Tacky the Penguin*. Ask the children to share opinions about the book.

Step 2: Ask for the names of the other penguins. What do those names tell you about these birds? A discussion of the meaning of "tacky" may be in order.

Step 3: Discuss the meaning of "odd bird." Explore some of the ways in which Tacky was different.

Small Group Instruction

Mix abilities for this session. Ask the children to find the following and read them aloud. They may work in pairs if it is helpful to the less able readers.

- Some sentences that tell how Tacky was different.

- Some sentences that tell facts about penguins.

- Some sentences that are completely fictional.

- The part about the hunters. Is any of this true? Support your answer.

Ask the students why hunters would want to capture penguins? Does the story support the answer?

Ask whether the children think it is fine to be different. Help them understand that although there are advantages to being an individual, it is also hard at times.

DAY 5

Feathers for Lunch

Shared Reading

Step 1: Review the story of Tacky.

Step 2: Look at the penguin fact chart. Read it together. Is there anything the children would change?

Step 3: Ask whether they now have answers to some of the questions. Are there some questions still unanswered?

Step 4: *Feathers for Lunch* is a delightful book that can be read in one session. Many of the birds included in the unit are featured in this book. Read it and discuss it briefly.

Small Group Instruction

Keep these sessions short to make time for a creative writing activity.

EL:

Step 1: Review vocabulary that was difficult in the first reading of the story.

Step 2: Assign parts of the story to read, or let the children choose them. The story can also be read as a play.

Step 3: Review the quotation mark and its importance in the reading of dialog.

Step 4: Read the book once or twice.

TL: Review the use of quotation marks. Then let this group read the story orally, either as a play or by individuals who choose their favorite parts. Encourage the children to use exaggerated expression as they read the dialog.

AL:

Step 1: Let this group decide how they would like to read the story: aloud, silently, as a play, or in some other way.

Step 2: Quickly review the use of quotation marks. Encourage dramatization of the dialog.

Step 3: Ask the children to write a question about penguins. When they have completed this assignment, bring them together and let them all read their questions. This can be a springboard for an excellent discussion. Remind the children to respond in a positive way to all questions.

Independent Activities

Materials

Penguin-shaped books for student writing

Paper and a variety of writing tools

Shape or large picture of a bird

Poster board cut into small cards

Velcro

Patterns of small penguins for tracing

White paper cut into the shape of a block of ice

Construction paper cut into bird shapes

Extension Activities

- Write questions, to be answered by others, about birds. These questions can be based on information learned from *Birds Are Animals* or from other books.

- Make a picture dictionary of winter birds. This may be more successful if the children work in groups or even as a whole class, depending on class size.

- Write creative penguin stories in penguin-shaped books.

- Write a factual penguin report, using materials in the classroom or from the school library.

- Make a story frame based on *Tacky the Penguin*. Fold a piece of 12-by-18-inch paper into fourths. ("Fold it once, fold it twice, fold it chicken soup with rice!") In the first box write the title and author, in the second box the names of the characters, in the third box state the problem, and in the final box tell how the problem was solved.

- Rewrite the story *Feathers for Lunch*. Change the cat to a different animal. Change the birds and plants to something else.

- Construct a diorama or triorama based on *Tacky the Penguin*.

Small Group and Center Activities

- Ask the entire group to brainstorm a list of winter words and write them on chart paper. Have each child choose a word, illustrate it, cut out the picture, and glue it beside the word on the chart. Place the chart in a writing center. Make available story paper, pencils, and crayons. Individually or with a partner, children are to write a sentence that uses one or more of the words and then illustrate it. These can be bound in a class "Winter" book and displayed in the classroom.

- Draw a large picture of a specific winter bird, or use a colored bird cutout (available in most card stores). Glue it to a piece of poster board. Write the body parts of the bird on small pieces of poster board. Fasten Velcro to the body parts on the picture and to the labels. The children must match the correct word to the body part and stick it on the picture.

- Cut out small penguin shapes. Write math facts on each and have partners solve them together. Cut out large blocks of ice, one for each player. When children solve a math fact correctly, they are to place a penguin on their iceberg.

- Vary the preceding activity by writing words, rather than math facts, on the penguins.

- Write bird riddles on cards or bird shapes. Place in a center along with bird books appropriate for the reading level of the class. Children can read the riddles and identify the birds, looking for help as necessary.

- Continue the bird-watching journal center.

Old Trail School is located in a national recreation park and there a wide variety of birds are attracted to bird feeders that are outside each classroom. We begin feeding birds on the first day of school and by the time we begin our study of winter birds there are usually many visitors. Our grounds staff continues to fill the feeders during winter break. Occasionally four-footed visitors visit the feeder also, and the children enjoy watching the way different animals move and solve the problem of getting to the food.

The shrubs outside the windows provide cover for sparrows during the cold weather. We are able to observe these little birds fluffing their feathers to stay warm. If a picture is worth a thousand words, this outdoor laboratory must be worth a million.

Science

Materials

Half-gallon milk carton

Yarn

Birdseed

Pine cones

Peanut butter

- If the children each made a bird book during this unit, continue writing and illustrating the final pages. Include a cover and put the books together with staples, a hole punch and yarn, or a binding machine. Encourage the students to decorate their covers, adding their own names as the author and illustrator. The name of the classroom or the school can be the publishing company. Students always enjoy making a dedication.

- Make a bird feeder from a half-gallon milk carton.

  Cut a rectangle in two sides of the carton.
  Punch a hole in the top of the carton. Tie a piece of yarn through it.
  Put birdseed in the bottom, and hang the feeder in a tree.

- Make bird treats as follows:

  Tie a piece of yarn around the top of a pine cone.
  Spread peanut butter on the cone.
  Place birdseed in a strong plastic bag; drop the cone inside the bag.
  Roll the pine cone around until it is covered with the seed.
  Take it out and tie it in the branches of a tree. Birds love it!

- Children can learn many things about birds through observation. If possible, place a feeder outside the classroom in a visible location away from the playground. As the children watch the birds come to the feeder, they can make observations and answer these questions:

  Are some birds more aggressive than others?
  Which birds perch on the feeder and which ones eat seeds from the ground?
  How do the birds move on branches and trunks of trees?
  Which are the most common birds that come to the feeder?

- Make a book about birds' beaks. Draw each one and describe it. List the kinds of birds that have this type of beak and the kinds of food they will eat.

- Make a book about the feet of birds. Ask the following questions:

  How many different kinds are there?
  How do different birds use their feet?
  What do we know about a bird by looking at its feet?

- Share the books with another class.

Math

- Make a graph of the various birds observed, by the day or the week. At the end of the unit, make a graph of the birds observed during the month of January.

- Conduct a survey of the class, the grade level, or families to determine which birds are the most popular. Graph the results. This can be done by grade level to show the favorite bird of first grade, second grade, and so on. Display the graphs in the hall, beginning with the kindergarten graph and ending with the oldest class in the school.

- This information can be analyzed in other ways, as follows:

  What was the favorite bird of most students?
  Did the students choose more winter birds or summer birds?
  Which bird was mentioned least?

- Encourage the use of math language by estimating and comparing the sizes of birds. Estimate the size of an emperor penguin, for example, and then research the actual size. Compare with other species of penguins and other birds studied. Encourage the use of vocabulary such as *greater than, less than, larger, smaller, taller,* and *shorter.* Students will enjoy working in small groups to make comparison charts, complete with pictures.

- Model story problems about penguins or other birds with the class. Partners can then work together to write and illustrate their own story problems. Upon completion, have them exchange the problems and solve them. Encourage them to write the equation at the bottom of the story. Take time to share the problems; then combine them into a class book.

Social Studies

- Read *Take a Trip to Antarctica.* Find Antarctica on a map or globe. Find the spot that marks the South Pole. Discuss the fact that this is the coldest and iciest region in the world. Ask the following questions:

  How could you get to Antarctica?
  What would you see there?
  What kind of things would you need to take with you?
  Do many people go there? Why or why not?

- Lead a discussion on bird migration. Point out that almost half of all bird species are migratory, spending summers in one place and then flying to another for the winter. With the assistance of the school librarian, help the children develop migratory routes for some common birds. Show the class the distance on a globe or map by pinning lengths of yarn across the route.

Foreign Language

- Translate the names of birds into French or the language being studied.

- Introduce the children to the parts of a bird in the foreign language.

- Translate one of the poems into the language, and read it frequently to the children. They will especially enjoy hearing "January" from *Chicken Soup with Rice* because they are so familiar with the format and the repetition.

Music

Creative Teaching Press, IC has a Big Book Kit with a musical cassette tape, *Little Color Birds,* available for purchase. Delightful birds introduce color words through their antics. The kit includes reproducible pages for individual student copies of the book.

Creative rhythmic activities based on the poem "The Penguin" are fun for the children. Help the children rewrite the poem to describe birds they have studied. Someone may be clever enough to think of a tune to go with his or her poem. Write a few on chart paper, and encourage the class to chant the words and/or clap them — like a rap. After the modeling activities, ask the children to write their own poems on story paper. Example:

> I am a bird you know quite well,
> All dressed in scarlet red.
> I have a great big thick beak
> And a crest upon my head.
> I get up very early,
> And sing out cheer, cheer, cheer.
> Get out of bed you sleepy head,
> A bright new day is here!   M.K.

They can then take turns reading the poems to their classmates to see whether they can identify the birds. Have the children illustrate the poems and display them on a bulletin board.

Art

- Have the children use crayons to create a winter scene on light blue or gray construction paper. This scene should include a tree, from which a bird feeder is hanging, and some winter birds. Dip a small sponge held with a clothespin into white paint and gently sponge snowflakes on the picture. When the pictures are dry, have the children put glue over the bird feeder and a little on the ground under it. While the glue is wet, they can place bird seed on it.

- Instead of using the sponges and paint, the children can dot their pictures with glue and sprinkle them with table salt or glitter to create "snow." Put the salt and the glitter in a shaker with large holes. When sprinkling the salt on the picture, they should put the picture into the lid of a large box so the extra salt can be caught and returned to the shaker.

- Roll a 12-by-18-inch sheet of black construction paper into a tube. Staple it together. This forms the body of a penguin. Cut heads, flippers, feet, and beaks from construction paper, and attach them with glue. Encourage the children to try to achieve a three-dimensional effect. Add a white breast cut from construction paper. The penguin can wear a scarf, hat, or other items the children might want to add.

- Create a bird from cut paper. Encourage the students to imagine a bird — the more whimsical the better. They are to cut the birds from assorted construction paper and glue them together. Ask the children to write brief descriptions of their birds. This is a good opportunity to talk about colorful words. Have them each name their bird and then tell where it lives, what it eats, and what it does for fun. Cut a large tree from brown paper; fasten it to a bulletin board. Position the birds and their stories on the bare branches of the tree. Make a label for the board that is also whimsical: perhaps "Our Tree-mendous Birds!"

Bibliography

Books

Bauer, Caroline Feller. *Snowy Day Stories and Poems*. New York: J. B. Lipincott, 1986.

Brett, Jan. *Annie and the Wild Animals*. Boston: Houghton Mifflin, 1985.

——. *The Mitten*. New York: Scholastic, 1990.

Briggs, Raymond. *The Snowman*. London: Hamish Hamilton, 1978. Reprint, New York: Scholastic, 1978.

——. *The Snowman Storybook*. New York: Random House, Inc., 1990.

Burton, Virginia Lee. *Katy and the Big Snow*. Boston: Houghton Mifflin, 1943.

Calhoun, Mary. *Cross Country Cat*. New York: Mulberry Books, 1986.

Carlson, Nancy. *Harriet and Walt*. Minneapolis: Carolrhoda Books, 1982.

Carlstrom, Nancy White. *Goodbye Geese*. New York: Scholastic, 1992.

Coleridge, Sara. *January Brings the Snow*. New York: Simon & Schuster, 1987.

Cowcher, Helen. *Antarctica*. New York: Farrar, Straus & Giroux West, 1991.

Ehlert, Lois. *Feathers For Lunch*. New York: Trumpet Club, 1990.

Florian, Douglas. *A Winter Day*. New York: Scholastic, 1991.

Greenfield, Eloise. *Rosa Parks*. New York: Thomas Y. Crowell, 1973.

Gundersheimer, Karen. *Happy Winter*. New York: Harper & Row, 1982.

Hader, Berta, and Elmer Hader. *The Big Snow*. New York: Scholastic, 1990.

Halloway, Judith, and Clive Harper. *Birds Are Animals*. Cleveland, Ohio: Modern Curriculum Press, 1990.

Henry, Marguerite. *Birds at Home*. Northbrook, Ill.: Hubbard Press, 1972.

Keats, Ezra Jack. *The Snowy Day*. New York: Scholastic, 1962.

——. *Whistle For Willie*. New York: Viking, 1964.

——. *Jennie's Hat*. New York: Harper & Row, 1966.

——. *Peter's Chair*. New York: Harper Trophy, Harper Collins , 1967.

——. *A Letter to Amy*. New York: Harper & Row, 1968.

——. *Goggles*. New York: Aladdin Books, Macmillan Publishing Co., 1969.

——. *Hi Cat*. New York: Macmillan, 1970.

——. *Apt II*. New York: Macmillan, 1971.

——. *Louie's Search*. New York: Greenwillow Books, William Morrow, 1975.

——. *The Trip*. New York: Greenwillow Books, 1978.

——. *Maggie and the Pirate*. New York: Macmillan, 1979.

——. *Regards to the Man in the Moon*. New York: Macmillan, 1981.

Kellogg, Steven, *The Mystery of the Old Red Mitten*. New York: Dial Books , 1974.

Lester, Helen. *Tacky the Penguin*. Boston: Houghton, Mifflin, 1988.

Lobe, Mira. *The Snowman Who Went For A Walk*. New York: William Morrow, 1984.

Marzolo, Jean. *Happy Birthday Martin Luther King*. New York: Scholastic, 1993.

Mastro, Betty. *Snow Day*. New York: Scholastic, 1989.

Morgan, Allen. *Sadie and the Snowman*. Toronto: Kids Can Press, 1985. Reprint, Scholastic, 1987.

Neitzel, Shirley. *The Jacket I Wear in the Snow*. New York: Greenwillow , William Morrow, 1989.

Stokes, Donald, and Lillian Stokes. *The Bird Feeder Book*. Boston: Little Brown, 1987.

Tresselt, Alvin. *The Mitten*. New York: Lathrop, Lee, and Shepard, 1964.

————. *White Snow, Bright Snow*. New York: Scholastic, 1988.

Wolff, Ashley. *A Year of Birds*. New York: Puffin Books, Dodd, Mead, 1984.

Wood, Audrey. *Little Penguin's Tale*. San Diego: Harcourt Brace Jovanovich, 1989.

Yolen, Jane. *Owl Moon*. New York: Philomel Books, Putnam & Grosset Group., 1987.

Ziefert, Harriet. *A New Coat for Anna*. New York: Alfred A. Knopf, 1986.

Poems

Aldis, Dorothy. "Snow." In *Time for Poetry,* edited by May Hill Arbuthnot. Chicago: Scott, Foresman, 1951.

Allen, Marie Louise. "First Snow." In *The Random House Book of Poetry for Children,* edited by Jack Prelutsky. New York: Random House, 1983.

———— "The Mitten Song." In *A New Treasury of Children's Poetry,* edited by JoAnna Cole. New York: Doubleday, 1984.

Bachmeister, Rhonda. "Icy." In *Read Aloud Poems for the Very Young,* edited by Jack Prelutsky. New York: Alfred Knopf, 1986.

Conkling, Hilda. "Chickadee." In *Time for Poetry,* edited by May Hill Arbuthnot. Chicago: Scott, Foresman, 1951.

de la Mare, Walter. "Crumbs." In *The Sound of Poetry,* edited by Mary C. Austin and Queenie B. Mills. Boston: Allyn and Bacon, 1963.

————. "The Snowflake." In *The Random House Book of Poetry for Children,* edited by Jack Prelutsky. New York: Random House, 1983.

Kuskin, Karla. "Snow." In *Snowy Day Stories and Poems,* edited by Caroline Feller Baver. New York: J.B. Lippincott, 1986.

Milne, A. A. "The More It Snows." In *The Random House Book of Poetry for Children,* edited by Jack Prelutsky. New York: Random House, 1983.

Ripp, Eleanor. "The Mitten Poem." In *The Mitten: Big Book Idea Book*. New York: Scholastic, 1992.

Sendak, Maurice. "January." In *Chicken Soup with Rice*. New York: Scholastic, 1987.

Sherman, Frank Dempster. "The Snow Bird." In *The Sound of Poetry,* edited by Mary C. Austin and Queenie B. Mills. Boston: Allyn and Bacon, 1963.

Tippet, James S. "Sh." In *Read-Together Poems,* edited by Helen A. Brown and Harry J. Heltman. New York: Harper & Row, 1961.

Tresselt, Alvin. "White Snow, Bright Snow." In *White Snow, Bright Snow.* New York: Scholastic, 1988.

Williams, Rozanne. "The Penguin." In *Theme Series: Snow.* Cypress, Calif.: Creative Teaching Press, 1990.

References

Commire, Anne. *Yesterday's Authors of Books for Children.* Detroit: Gale Research Company, 1977.

Kovacs, Deborah and James Preller. *Meet The Authors and Illustrators.* Vol. 1. New York: Scholastic, 1991.

————. *Meet the Authors and Illustrators.* Vol. 2. New York: Scholastic, 1993.

Norby, Shirley and Gregory Ryan. *Famous Children's Authors.* Minneapolis: T.S. Denison, 1988.

3
FEBRUARY

Theme: Love Your Body

The instructional focus this month is a health unit about the human body. Children learn about the function of the heart, lungs, intestines, bones, and skin. It is not expected that they will master all that is presented, but each will learn according to his or her individual abilities.

The holidays of this month are addressed through books and poems and in a short unit on chocolate.

Week 1: Overview

Instructional Books

Strega Nona by Tomie dePaola
Big Anthony and the Magic Ring by Tomie dePaola

Related Titles

It's Groundhog Day by Steven Kroll (to be read aloud)
If You Give a Mouse a Cookie by Laura Joffe Numeroff
If You Give a Moose a Muffin by Laura Joffe Numeroff
Gregory the Terrible Eater by Mitchell Sharmat

Poems

"Ground Hog Day" by Lilian Moore
"February" by Maurice Sendak
"Spaghetti" by Shel Silverstein

Objectives

1. **Phonetic skills**
   Begin to understand the endings er, est, and ed.
2. **Comprehension**
   Begin to understand the concept of categorizing.
3. **Alphabetizing skills**
   Learn to alphabetize to the second letter.

Materials

Word cards in the shape of a pasta pot

Drawing paper

Writing paper

Poetry and Skills Session

DAY 1

"February"

Step 1: The children will anticipate the content of this poem. Invite predictions before showing it.

Step 2: Suggest that the children who have a birthday in February read the poem together.

Step 3: Ask how this poem is like others from *Chicken Soup with Rice*.

Step 4: Ask for other ideas for the final two lines of the poem.

Step 5: Read the poem again for fun.

DAY 2

"Ground Hog Day"

The purpose for including this poem is to observe Groundhog Day, February 2. Use this as a springboard for the discussion of the day, for the anticipation of spring, and to evaluate superstitions.

Is there any scientific basis for the theory that if the groundhog sees his shadow it means more winter? Encourage a discussion. Suggest that the class count the days until the weather warms to see whether the groundhog's "prediction" was accurate.

DAY 3

"Spaghetti"

Step 1: Introduce this poem by asking the children to name types of pasta. Begin a chart with these names. Ask the children to bring samples and paste them next to the appropriate name. Continue adding to the chart during the unit.

Step 2: Read the poem together.

Step 3: Inquire about the ways the class likes to eat spaghetti. Suggest that they bring their favorite recipe to school.

Step 4: Briefly review vowel sounds by asking volunteers to identify them in the words of the poem.

DAY 4

Step 1: Reread the poem from the previous day.

Step 2: Add new kinds of pasta to the chart.

Step 3: Ask the children to share the recipes they have brought to class. Compare the ingredients. Encourage comments about spaghetti, cooking it, and eating it.

DAY 5

Let the children choose poems to read individually or with a friend.

Reading Instruction

DAY 1

Biographical sketch of Tomie dePaola

Tomie dePaola was born September 15, 1934, in Meriden, Connecticut. He grew up in the days before television and learned to visualize pictures while listening to the radio and to his mother reading stories. He informed his first grade teacher that he was going to make picture books when he grew up. His first book was a birthday present for his sister Maureen (Commire 1971).

It is Mr. dePaola's philosophy that you can write anywhere, and indeed he has written first drafts of stories in unusual places, including airplanes. Although he can write in uncommon places, the illustrations are done only in his studio.

He has always been interested in folk tales, although their origin is not important. It is Mr. dePaola's belief that writings from the past tell us important things about ourselves and our lives. The ideas that come into a person's head should be explored to see if they are good ones. It is his conviction that adults should not comment on an idea. When an idea occurs, it should be pursued.

Mr. dePaola's books usually draw upon his own childhood experiences. One of his books, *The Art Lesson*, is a true story that he told an editor. The editor encouraged him to put it into a book, which he did (Kovacs & Preller 1991). Look for a heart in the pictures by Mr. dePaola because that is his "autograph." He loves to get mail and, indeed, receives so much that he has a secretary to take care of it. One of his favorite foods is popcorn, and children often bring it to him when he attends an autograph session at a book store (Norby & Ryan 1988).

Strega Nona

Shared Reading

Display the big book of *Strega Nona*.

- Step 1: Read the biographical sketch of Tomie dePaola. Tell the class that his grandparents came from Italy.
- Step 2: Locate Italy on a map or globe. Assess the students' knowledge of the country.
- Step 3: Follow the usual procedure for making predications about the story. Check them at the end of the session.

Step 4: Read the first few pages with the children. When they have heard enough of the story to understand that magic is involved, stop and discuss it. What kind of magic do they believe in? What about magic tricks? Magic words?

Step 5: Continue reading the story, allowing time for comments from the children.

Small Group Instruction

During this session, mix all abilities for directed reading activities. Have the children read the book, one or two pages at a time, and pause for discussion of the story and the illustrations. As always, immediately supply words that are difficult for the less able readers or allow them to ask a friend.

DAY 2

Strega Nona

Shared Reading

Step 1: Review the story, the location of Italy, and the use of magic in the plot.

Step 2: Ask the children to name other stories that have a theme of magic in the plot. They will probably suggest *Cinderella, Snow White,* and *Rumpelstiltskin* among others. Provide plenty of time for this discussion.

Step 3: Reread the story, encouraging comments about the characters and illustrations.

Step 4: Help the children select the vocabulary on which they will focus during the week. Write the words on cards or paper cut in the shape of pasta pots.

Small Group Instruction

EL:

Step 1: Spread the vocabulary cards on the reading table. Ask each child to select a card, read it, and use the word in a sentence. Continue taking turns until all words have been read.

Step 2: If the reading level of *Strega Nona* is frustrating for this group, help them retell the story. Write their version on the chalkboard; later transfer it to paper and copy it for use by the group during the week.

Step 3: Sequence the events of the story, focusing on the actions of Strega Nona and Big Anthony.

TL: Have the students find the vocabulary words in the story and read the passage aloud. Ask the following questions:

- Were the townspeople responsible in any way for Big Anthony's disobeying Strega Nona? Why or why not?

- Did Big Anthony behave like an adult?

- Is this story believable?

At the end of the session, make time for the children to read the story with a friend.

AL:

Step 1: Distribute copies of *Big Anthony and the Magic Ring*. Allow time for the group to read the story silently, assisting with new words as needed.

Step 2: Discuss the story. Compare it to *Strega Nona*. Is the setting the same? Are the characters the same? Ask how they would have known that the story was written and illustrated by Tomie dePaola.

DAY 3

Strega Nona

Shared Reading

Review the meaning of "folk tale." Remind the students that *The Mitten* was a Ukrainian folk tale. Ask them the following questions:

- What lessons can one learn from a folk tale?

- What lesson did Big Anthony learn in the story?

- Were there lessons for other people in the book?

EL:

Step 1: Distribute copies of the version of *Strega Nona* that the group wrote during the previous session. Review the vocabulary. Hold up a vocabulary card, asking someone to read a sentence in the story that contains that word. Continue until all have had at least one turn.

Step 2: Ask a volunteer to read the most exciting (happiest, funniest, silliest) part of the story.

Step 3: Discuss the ending of the words in step 2: "est." Extend the discussion to include "er."

Step 4: Review and reinforce decoding skills that need attention.

Step 5: Have each child read the story with a partner.

Step 6: Ask the students to illustrate their story. Collect the papers. They will be placed in a cover to be decorated by each child and taken home at the end of the week. Use this for an informal comprehension check.

TL: Begin this session with a review and reinforcement of decoding skills that apply to the target vocabulary. Encourage the children to share ways in which they have decoded new words. Write five words on the board that will probably be new to the group. Apply the decoding strategies to these words.

Ask each child to choose a favorite page from the book to read aloud.

AL:

Step 1: Review the story of *Big Anthony and the Magic Ring*. Encourage the children to think creatively about other problems that misuse of the ring might have caused.

Step 2: Ask what other magic things Strega Nona might have in the chest. What kind of magic would these items work? Encourage elaboration.

Step 3: Tell the group that you are going to give each of them something from the chest and they must describe what happens when the magic works. The items may be named or, if time permits, you can gather a number of things and pass them out. Some possible items are a pen, pair of glasses, measuring cup, spoon, shoe, button, safety pin, small stone, nail, and bottle of glue.

Distribute paper on which the children are to draw pictures of what happens when the magic of their item is working. They may either write the story or tell it to the group during the next session.

DAY 4

Shared Reading

Pose a hypothetical situation that illustrates cause and effect. Example: You wake up on Monday morning, look out the window, and see that there has been a snowfall during the night. You remember that you left your snow boots at school on Friday. What will happen?

Help the children plot a series of possible events: Their feet will get wet going to school. Their mothers will be upset with them. They will be uncomfortable in school because their feet are wet. Relate this to the events in *Strega Nona*, and discuss the events that caused repercussions. Someone may mention *If You Give a Mouse a Cookie* as an excellent example of cause and effect.

Small Group Instruction

EL:

- Plan a cloze activity for this session. Review the vocabulary before beginning. Write sentences on the board, leaving blanks for the target vocabulary. Ask individuals to read a sentence, choose the word that is missing, and place it in the blank. At the conclusion of the session, read the new version of the story that the students have written and let the children show their illustrations.

- Distribute construction paper to be used for book jackets. Have the children design their own covers.

TL:

Step 1: Display the vocabulary on the table. Allow students to take turns placing the words in alphabetical order.

Step 2: Ask each child to choose a word, tell something about it that relates to a phonetic rule (i.e. it has a short a, long o, and so on), and use the word in a sentence.

Step 3: Have each child read the story with a friend.

AL: The students share their magic stories during this session. After each has had a turn, let the group choose one of the items and write a cooperative story about it. Record the story and make individual copies to be illustrated.

DAY 5

Creative Writing

Devote the reading time to creative writing. Discuss *Strega Nona* and the cause-and-effect theme. Make suggestions as needed to help motivate the children's writing. It is appropriate to write on the board some words that the students think they might use in the story. This technique often removes blocks for children who are not yet confident writers. Some motivating questions might be as follows:

- Which character in the story is most like yourself? Tell why.

- There is a big problem at the end of the story: the town is covered with pasta. What are some ways the people could get rid of all of it? Be creative!

- What would have happened if Strega Nona had used the pot for soup instead of pasta?

- Would you like to have Strega Nona for a friend? Why or why not?

- Would you like to have Big Anthony for a friend? Why or why not?

Some children may wish to use individual items from Strega Nona's chest as the basis for their story. The class will have listened to the AL group as they discussed and shared their stories and may be motivated by one of their ideas. Any idea that stimulates creative thinking is acceptable.

Independent Activities

Materials

Drawing paper

Writing paper

Assorted dry pasta

Small cards with the letters from "spaghetti" written one per card

Extension Activities

- Children have probably seen posters for lost animals. Tell them that Big Anthony has been lost and they need to help find him. Design a poster of Big Anthony that includes his picture and gives a description of him. Help them determine what this description should include, writing the key words on the board (height, weight, clothes, and so on).

- Make a cartoon of the town of Calabria. Bring some examples of cartoons from a Sunday edition of the local newspaper so the children will have a model. Have the children draw the townspeople, and show them how to use speech balloons. Encourage them to write what each person is saying about Strega Nona and/or Big Anthony. The class can work in small groups, with each child adding a successive part to a longer story.

- Big Anthony has a problem following directions. Write a letter to him, suggesting some changes in his behavior and telling him why it would be good for him to follow these suggestions.

- Write a verse for the magic objects used with the AL group during sessions 3 and 4.

- Plan a pasta party. Ask a parent or a chef from a local restaurant to demonstrate the making of pasta. Definitely eat the pasta!

Small Group and Center Activities

- Place construction paper, glue, and an assortment of pasta in small dishes in a center. The children are to glue the pasta to the paper to create pasta pictures. They can use markers to color the pasta and the background.

- Write a menu for a restaurant that serves only pasta. What new recipes could be invented?

- Glue three pasta pots to a piece of tag board or other heavy paper. Leave the top of the pots free, thus forming pockets. Write words from *Strega Nona* on paper shaped like pasta. Label the pots *nouns, verbs,* and *adjectives.* Let the children sort the words accordingly.

- Write the individual letters from *pasta* or *spaghetti* on small cards. Place them on a table with writing paper cut in the shape of a pasta pot. The children are to arrange the letters to form new words, recording the words on the paper.

Science

- Have the children compare dry pasta with the same kind after it has been cooked. Compare the weight, length, width, taste, color, flexibility, and other attributes that the children might suggest.

- Determine what happens to cooked pasta after it dries. Does it return to the original shape?

Math

- Measure different kinds of pasta. Which is the longest, and how can it be measured?

- Determine which ways of serving pasta are favored by the class. Make a graph to show individual choices.

- Write story problems using the characters in *Strega Nona*. Example: *Strega Nona invited four friends for pasta. Big Anthony invited two friends. How many friends did they serve? How many people were there altogether?*

- Use pasta to work with fractions. Break a piece of spaghetti in half. Are the pieces equal? If not, is it accurate to say that each is one-half?

- Compare recipes for cooking pasta. Is the time the same in each? If not, why not?

- Estimate how long it will take a pot of water to reach boiling. Bring a pot of water to a boil, and compare the time with the estimates. Help the children conclude that time relates to the size of the pot and the quantity of water.

Social Studies

- Locate Calabria on the globe or a world map. Note the shape of Italy. What direction is Italy from Paris? From the home town of the class?

- Ask the students how Madeline would travel if she were going to Calabria.

- Ask one or two volunteers to look in an encyclopedia, read about Italy, and share the information with the class.

- Invite a community resource person to speak to the class about Italy. The person could discuss holidays, perhaps reviewing some of the information covered during December's study of holidays.

Foreign Language

Introduce several common Italian words to the class in addition to *grazi,* which is in the book. Examples: *pasta, spaghetti, spumoni,* and *parmesan.*

Music

Play music by Italian composers during this unit. *The Barber of Seville* has songs that will delight young children. Also the "Tarantella" may be familiar. If not, it will be after they hear it several times!

Art

Ask each child to bring a shoe box to school. It will be the basis for a diorama of a spaghetti restaurant. Students can use construction paper to create a background, furniture, and people. Have them make a pot of clay, using a pencil to put a hole in the bottom of the pot. They will thread a long piece of yarn through the bottom of the pot and place the pot in the diorama, thus producing the pasta pot that would not stop cooking. Encourage children to use their imaginations for this activity.

Week 2: Overview

This week will probably precede, or perhaps include, Valentine's Day. Combine this loving holiday with the study of chocolate. The week is enriched by giving the children small (and yes, unhealthy!) chocolate treats. A bag of Hershey's Kisses will go a long way. The authors have also given pencils that have the names of chocolate candy and smell like chocolate.

Instructional Books

The Skeleton Inside You by Philip Balestrino
Valentine Bears by Eve Bunting
The Big Block of Chocolate by Janet Slater Redhead
Valentine Friends by Ann Schweninger
A Book about Your Skeleton by Ruth Gross

Related Titles

Bread and Jam for Frances by Russell Hoban
Breakfast Buffalo by Susan D. McClanahan

Poems

"Chocolate, Chocolate" by Arnold Adoff
"If I Were a Valentine" by Kathleen Eiland
"The Reason I Like Chocolate" by Nikki Giovanni
"Chocolate Cake" by Nina Payne

Objectives

1. **Phonetic skills**
   Review and reinforce endings and root words.
2. **Structural analysis**
   Review pronouns.
   Begin to understand the concept of syllables (dividing between double consonants).
   Review synonyms and antonyms.
3. **Comprehension**
   Review the concepts of main idea and supporting facts.

Materials

Chocolate candy kisses

Word cards on brown construction paper cut in the shape of a chocolate kiss

Books in the shape of a chocolate kiss for student writing

Poetry and Skills Session

DAY 1

"Chocolate Cake"

Step 1: Ask a volunteer to read the name of the poem. Ask whether everyone in the class likes chocolate cake. Allow time for discussion. It is possible that some child is allergic to chocolate or has a friend who is, and this adds another dimension to the discussion.

Step 2: Read the poem to the children, encouraging those who wish to join in.

Step 3: Briefly discuss the rhythm of the poem. Read it again with the class, clapping in time to the words.

Step 4: Ask children to think about the main idea of this poem. What is the author saying?

Step 5: Ask the students to find words in the poem that have a root word with an ending. Examples: *sifted, lifted, caked,* and *baked.* Help children "separate" root words from endings. Change the beginning sound of *cake* to form a new word. This is a reteaching strategy that will help students who still have not mastered the concept of "word families." If some are still struggling with this, continue the activity in a small group.

DAY 2

"Chocolate, Chocolate"

Step 1: Quickly reread the poem from the previous session.

Step 2: Introduce today's poem by pointing to the title and asking whether the two poems are the same.

Step 3: Read the poem together, taking time to interpret the content. Could someone really "marry" chocolate? What does the poet mean?

Step 4: Ask what other flavors are favorites besides chocolate?

Step 5: Discuss the main idea of the poem.

Step 6: Ask the children to identify the pronouns in the poem. Observant children will quickly note that there are no capital letters in this poem and that the form is different. Use this opportunity to discuss freedom in the form of poetry. This is a good opportunity to read a few of e. e. cummings's poems and point out that he also is unconventional when composing. Point out that authors of prose do not have this option.

Step 7: Read the poem again for fun.

DAY 3

"The Reason I Like Chocolate"

Step 1: Read the name of the poem, and ask for an interpretation of the title. Ask the children whether they like chocolate and why.

Step 2: Read the poem to the children, asking them to follow the words. Read it again as they listen with their eyes closed, visualizing what the poem is saying. After a brief discussion of the content, ask again how the title pertains to the poem.

Step 3: Ask what facts support the idea that the author likes chocolate.

Step 4: Many words in this poem have double consonants. This is a good opportunity to discuss how words with double consonants break into syllables: between the double letters. This concept may be difficult for the less mature children, but many in the class will quickly master the concept.

Step 5: Read the poem again for pleasure.

DAY 4

"If I Were a Valentine"

Step 1: The rhythm of this poem makes it fun for the children to read together. Read it to the class; then invite them to join in.

Step 2: Suggest that they sing it, using the tune to "The Muffin Man."

Step 3: Briefly point out the different kinds of sentences: telling and asking. Review the punctuation at the end of each.

Step 4: Close the session by singing the poem.

DAY 5

Each child can choose a poem and read it individually or with a friend.

Reading Instruction

DAY 1

The Big Block of Chocolate

Shared Reading

Step 1: Introduce *The Big Block of Chocolate* in the usual manner.

Step 2: Ask for comments about the style of the illustrations. They are different from those in other books the children have read. The students should make some comparisons with artists such as Eric Carle, Ezra Jack Keats, and other favorites.

Step 3: Read the story, using exaggerated expressions in the lines, " . . . it's mine, and all for me. I savor every bite of it . . . " The children will enjoy the idea of hiding the chocolate to avoid sharing it. Encourage them to tell about a time when they had something they did not want to share.

Step 4: With the class, decide which words will be targeted during the week. Write these words on brown construction paper cut into the shape of chocolate kisses.

Small Group Instruction

Mix abilities for the small groups. Reread the story, pausing for comments about the pictures and the content. Use directed reading strategies as appropriate for the children in the group.

DAY 2

The Big Block of Chocolate

Shared Reading

Step 1: Review the content of the story. Ask the children to think about the main idea of the book. What theme goes through the story, and what is the consequence of the theme? (selfishness and loss of the candy) Discuss the supporting facts.

Step 2: Direct a discussion that focuses on the cause and effect of selfishness. Encourage the children to conclude that the characters who enjoyed the chocolate were the ants who were eager to share.

Step 3: Ask who knows the meaning of "savor." Tell the class that they will perform an experiment to help with this definition. Give each child one Hershey's Kiss. Tell them to eat it as quickly as possible. Talk about the taste and how much they enjoyed it. Give them a second candy, and ask them to let it melt slowly in their mouth. As it is dissolving, talk about the feeling of the chocolate on the tongue and its flavor. Then ask which way provided the most enjoyment. This is the meaning of "savor."

> We had a birthday treat a few days after this 'experiment' and several children said, "Oh, I'm going to s-a-v-o-r this!" They began using this word in daily conversations, sometimes with great humor. Later in the year, one child informed a teacher during recess that she would "s-a-v-o-r" the beautiful spring day.

Small Group Instruction

EL and **TL** work together in this session. Write the following questions on the chalkboard. Children are to work with a partner to locate the answers in the text.

- How did Jenny and the animals feel about chocolate?

- In what order did the animals find the chocolate?

- What did the sun do to the chocolate? Why?

- How can you prove that the ants liked the chocolate?

- Who was the most selfish? How can you prove this?

After the children have found the answers, discuss the questions one at a time, encouraging them to read the part of the text that supports their answers.

AL: This group will pursue a research activity this week. Coordinate times with the school librarian so that the children can work without disturbing others and get help if it is needed.

Working in pairs, they are to look in encyclopedias and other sources to find the answers to the following questions:

- How does chocolate grow?

- How is it manufactured?

- Who first used chocolate?

- When and how was chocolate first used in candy?

- What countries produce the most chocolate?

- What country uses the most chocolate?

- What are the different kinds of chocolate?

Ask students to name as many chocolate things as possible. To get started, they can think of cookies and cakes. (This will overlap with the shared reading activity in the next session, but that is acceptable.)

The students will need most of the week to complete this activity.

DAY 3

The Big Block of Chocolate

Shared Reading

- Invite the children to read the story as a play. Assign speaking parts to various groups, and ask one child to be the "book," or narrator.

- Distribute the vocabulary words among the children. Then ask each to stand, read his or her word, and use it in a sentence. Have the student identify the root and ending of the word. If this is a problem for any of the children, let them ask other students for help.

- Discuss the parts (syllables) of a word. Read a number of words, clapping on the syllables.

Small Group Instruction

EL:

Step 1: Review the vocabulary. Reinforce decoding skills as needed.

Step 2: Ask students to choose their favorite character. Let one or two students, depending on the size of the group, be the narrator.

Step 3: Read the book as a play. Encourage the children to follow so they can begin reading their parts without a cue from you. During this reading, observe students who are having difficulty. Meet with them individually to address their needs.

TL:

Step 1: Review the vocabulary. Work on phonetic skills that need reinforcement.

Step 2: Have the students put the vocabulary in alphabetical order. Review the process to be used when a word begins with the same letter(s) as other words.

Step 3: Isolate the adjectives, write each on the board, and ask the group for other words that mean the same thing. Write the synonyms under the initial word.

Step 4: Follow the oral reading procedure of the preceding group.

AL: Bring the group together to discuss their progress on the "chocolate report." Ask them to share their sources of information.

Encourage those who are not working at an appropriate pace to ask for help if needed. Discuss the amount of work assigned, and help the children set daily goals so that the assignment will be completed on time.

DAY 4

Valentine Bears

Shared Reading

Step 1: Introduce this book in the usual manner.

Step 2: Read the story to the class. Encourage discussion about the content and the illustrations.

Step 3: Compare the actual story with the predictions. Evaluate the ideas that did not fit in the story. Ask whether they could be the basis for a new story.

Step 4: Ask whether anyone heard a word in the story that had an er or est ending. Write these words on the chalkboard.

Small Group Instruction

EL:

Step 1: Review the story with the children.

Step 2: Write words that may be troublesome on the board, discussing decoding strategies.

Step 3: Using directed reading questions, have the group read the book one or two pages at a time. At the conclusion, ask each student to choose a partner; let them read the story to each other.

TL:

Step 1: Write on the board five or six words from the story. Ask the children to think of words that mean the opposite of these words. Write the antonyms under the associated words.

Step 2: Have this group read the book, a few pages at a time. Ask content questions. Note words that cause problems.

Step 3: Write the difficult words on the board and discuss strategies for decoding them. Involve the students in this so that they can learn from each other.

Step 4: Have the group choose partners and let them read the story to each other.

AL: The research project should be nearing completion. Assess the progress of the group and assist as needed. As the students are preparing their reports, help them use topic sentences and supporting facts. This will give them a form for organizing the information they have found.

Make *Valentine Bears* available to those who wish to read it independently.

DAY 5

Shared Reading

Step 1: Discuss what has been learned about chocolate during this week. Have the AL group share their research with the class. Allow time for questions and discussion.

Step 2: Look at the chart on which the children have listed the names of foods that contain chocolate. Read it together. Add other suggestions to the list.

Step 3: Insert the word "chocolate" in the titles of some favorite stories and ask volunteers to suggest a brief plot. Examples: "King Midas and the Chocolate Touch," "Little Chocolate Riding Hood," and "Peter Rabbit Visits Mr. MacGregor's Chocolate Factory." After the children have had fun with these ideas, tell them that they are to write their own chocolate story. They may use one of these ideas or a new one.

Step 4: Distribute writing paper that has been cut in the shape of a large chocolate kiss. When the story is compete, give each child brown construction paper cut in the same shape to be made into covers for the books. Aluminum foil can also be used for this purpose.

Independent Activities

Materials

Construction paper

Cards on which pairs of synonyms and antonyms have been written

Letters from the word "chocolate" written on small cards

Wooden tongue depressors for puppets

Extension Activities

- Miss Jenny is upset about the loss of her chocolate bar. Tell the students that they are her good friends and want to help her. Each student must write a letter to help her feel better.

- Make a sequence strip about *The Big Block of Chocolate*. Fold 12-by-18-inch paper in half (a "hot dog fold") and then in half again to make four boxes. Cut down the center of the paper, and glue the two strips together. Number the boxes, using both sides of the paper. Draw pictures of the story in sequence. Write a few words to identify the picture.

- Using a literature square, write a word on the outside flap and a rhyming word on the inside. Illustrate both words.

- Invent a new chocolate bar. With the class, make a list of ingredients that can be added to chocolate. Place this list in a prominent place. The children then combine several of these ingredients with chocolate, draw a picture, and name their invention. The candy bar can be designed with brown construction paper and pasted on the paper. Display these on a bulletin board with a catchy title, such as "Delicious Inventions."

- Place a bag of chocolate treats on the desk at the beginning of the morning. At some time, hide them. Ask the class to write a story about what could have happened to the treats. Have the children share their stories with the class. Naturally the bag will reappear and be savored by the class!

Small Group and Center Activities

- Write a list of synonyms on brown paper and a list of antonyms on white. Match the words. The color code will help the children see that synonyms have similar meanings and antonyms have the opposite.

- How many different words can small groups of children make from the letters in "chocolate"? Using a brown crayon, record the words on paper in the shape of a chocolate kiss.

- Make puppets of the characters in *The Big Block of Chocolate*. Attach them to wooden tongue depressors, and make a play of the story.

- Cut a number of hearts out of red construction paper. Write a root word on one half and an ending on the other half. Cut the center in jagged lines. The students are to put the puzzles together and record the words on a piece of heart-shaped writing paper, using a red writing instrument. Store these hearts in a valentine candy box.

Science

Step 1: Introduce the study of the human body by reading *The Skeleton Inside You*. For this unit, use *Learning about Your Body,* a book available through the Frank Schaffer Company. The photocopy masters parallel the themes in this unit and, when finished, form a big book that the children can take home.

Step 2: Put a Halloween skeleton on a bulletin board. Label the bones, following the chart at the back of *A Book about Your Skeleton*. These skeletons are accurate reproductions of the human body and a good tool for teaching children the names of the bones.

Step 3: Define the skeleton and its purpose.

Step 4: Discuss the various kinds of joints that allow the body to move.

Step 5: Discuss the fact that muscles move the bones by pulling. Muscles cannot push.

Step 6: Discuss the function of the digestive system, which breaks food down into small particles that the blood takes to all parts of the body.

Step 7: Discuss the function of the heart as it relates to the respiratory system. It is the pump that makes the blood circulate. The American Heart Association has excellent materials for classroom teachers. The study of the heart ties in nicely with Valentine's Day.

Math

Materials

Chocolate bars

- Divide three large chocolate candy bars into half, fourths, and thirds. The class participates by drawing the candy on paper, using lines to show the division, and labeling the fractions. To vary this activity, pass out precut pieces of brown paper. Have the class cut them into fractions, glue them to another sheet of paper, and label the parts.

- Write story problems about buying candy. Example: *If Miss Jenny bought two chocolate bars for 10 cents each, how much did she spend?* Combine these into a class book. If there is more than one section of the grade in the school, the books can be exchanged with another section.

Foreign Language

Translate candy-related words into the language being studied. Ask children questions in the language. Example: "Do you like chocolate?" The child is to respond in the language, "Yes (or no) I (don't) like chocolate."

Art

Materials

Chocolate pudding

Paper for finger painting

- Distribute dampened finger-painting paper. Give each child a small cup of instant chocolate pudding to be used as finger paint.

- Ask the children to bring candy wrappers to school. Begin collecting them in advance of the time they will be needed. The wrappers can be used for a variety of purposes: as a collage of a large candy bar, to form the shape of a body (face and details to be added with crayons or markers), or to make a valentine card.

Week 3: Overview

Instructional Books

The Magic Schoolbus: Inside the Human Body by Joanna Cole
More Spaghetti, I Say by Rita Golden Gellman
Why Can't I Fly? by Rita Golden Gellman

Related Titles

A Monkey Grows Up by Rita Golden Gellman (to be read aloud)
The Hungry Thing by Jan Slepian and Ann Seidler (to be read aloud or more
    capable readers can read silently)
The Hungry Thing Returns by Jan Slepian and Ann Seidler
Learning about Your Body by Lori Freeberg

Poems

"My Mouth" by Arnold Adoff
"Celery" by Ogden Nash
"I'm Hungry" by Jack Prelutsky
"Jellyfish Stew" by Jack Prelutsky

Objectives

1. **Phonetic skills**
   Begin to understand vowel diphthongs.

2. **Structural skills**

Review nouns, pronouns, verbs, adjectives, and any other skills that need such a review.

3. **Comprehension**

Review the concept of main idea.

Begin to recognize topic sentences.

Materials

Word cards shaped like bowls

12-by-18-inch newsprint

Writing paper

Poetry and Skills Session

DAY 1

"I'm Hungry"

Step 1: Introduce the poem by inviting a volunteer to read the title. Discuss how children feel before lunch. Encourage the children to name foods they may want when they are hungry. Is anyone ever hungry for broccoli? liver? squash?

Step 2: Read the poem. Ask the students to name the foods in the poem. Ask which foods are real and which have been used for humor. What does "fillet" mean? Read the poem again, inviting children to join the reading. Allow time for discussion and enjoyment of Mr. Prelutsky's humor.

Step 3: Read the poem again for fun. Distribute copies of the poem for your students to illustrate and include in their poetry notebooks.

DAY 2

"My Mouth"

Step 1: Ask the children to look at the poem and identify what is different about it. They will notice the form and the lack of capitals. Ask whether this is the first time they have seen a poem written this way. They may remember "Chocolate, Chocolate," read during the chocolate unit. Display it beside "My Mouth" to help the children see that they are written by the same poet.

Step 2: Read the poem, inviting the children to join in when they feel comfortable.

Step 3: Discuss the meaning of the poem.

Step 4: Review the long sound of i, e, o, and a by asking individuals to find words that contain these sounds. Mark them with an erasable pen.

Step 4: Read the poem again with the children, for fun.

DAY 3

"Celery"

Step 1: Before the poem is read, distribute small pieces of celery to the children. As they eat, ask them to think about the sounds they hear and the way the vegetable feels in their mouths. Encourage all students to describe the taste, sound, and feel.

Step 2: List adjectives that the children have used.

Step 3: Read the poem "Celery." Compare the poem to what they just experienced.

Step 4: Initiate a discussion of how the cooking process changes celery. If time and facilities allow, cook some celery and compare it to the raw form.

Step 5: Review the aw and ew combinations.

Step 6: Read the poem again. Distribute copies of the poem for your students to illustrate and include in their poetry notebooks.

DAY 4

"Jellyfish Stew"

Step 1: Introduce the poem by telling the class that it was written by Jack Prelutsky. Invite speculation about a stew made of jellyfish. Children should identify the jellyfish as an animal that lives in the oceans, and they may wish to share an experience they have had with the animal. The discussion should then be directed to the kinds of seafood that they enjoy eating.

Step 2: Read the poem. Compare the instructions to other methods for preparing seafood. The students will quickly point out that this is a fictional food.

Step 3: Ask if anyone suspected that it would be a "silly" poem when they heard the author was Jack Prelutsky? Briefly discuss other poems by Mr. Prelutsky with which they are familiar.

Step 4: Have the children read the poem several times.

DAY 5

Today is for shared reading of favorite poems by individuals or small groups.

Reading Instruction

DAY 1

Biographical sketch of Rita Gelman

Rita Gelman was born on July 2, 1937, in Bridgeport, Connecticut. She went to college in California and married a sports writer. They had two children, Mitchell and Jan. Among the books she has published are *Why Can't I Fly?* and *More Spaghetti, I Say*. She has also written sports stories with her husband (Commire 1971).

More Spaghetti, I Say

Shared Reading

Step 1: Introduce the book in the usual manner by asking for predictions.

Step 2: Read the biographical sketch of Rita Gellman.

Step 3: Read the book, inviting the class to join in when they wish and encouraging comments as the story unfolds.

Step 4: Compare the story with the predictions. If no one mentions that this is a circle story, point it out to the class.

Step 5: Read the story again, with the boys reading Freddie's part and the girls reading Minnie's. Make note of the words that appear to be new or difficult. Write these words on cards shaped like bowls for later use in small group instruction.

Small Group Instruction

Combine the children in small groups, mixing abilities, and read the story as a play. One child takes the part of the narrator, one is Minnie, and one is Freddie. After several pages have been read, change actors so that everyone has a turn. Encourage dramatization by complimenting those who read with a great deal of expression. Do not make children feel uncomfortable if they are unable to be dramatic; it is easier for some than others.

Be alert for difficult words, and address these in the next small group session.

DAY 2

More Spaghetti, I Say

Shared Reading

Step 1: Review the story from the previous session. Briefly discuss the main idea and supporting facts.

Step 2: Ask the students to name the ways Minnie liked to eat spaghetti. Record the ways on the chalkboard or chart paper. Invite the children to help spell the words.

Step 3: Read the story again, asking the children to take different parts. Perhaps this time they can decide which part they wish to read. Look at the list written before the second reading. Were any ways omitted? If so, record them now.

Step 4: Ask the children to think of some other ways Minnie and Freddie could eat spaghetti. Encourage creative thinking.

Small Group Instruction

EL:

Step 1: Begin with a review of the vocabulary words. Ask the children to choose their favorite page in the book and read it aloud. Make note of words that cause difficulty. At the end of the oral reading, put these words on the board and have the children share ways they found to decode them.

Step 2: Have the children make small books in which they will write and illustrate the words that are difficult for them. The books can be in the shape of a bowl, a rectangle that represents a box of pasta, or another shape that appeals to the group.

TL:

Step 1: Write the lines from pages 12 and 13 on the board, omitting the nouns. Ask the group to turn to these pages and read them aloud.

Step 2: Tell the group that they are going to make some new lines for the book, and ask for suggestions for other ways to eat the spaghetti. Record their suggestions.

Step 3: Call attention to the rhyming of the second and fourth lines and the sixth and eighth. Help the children decide upon words that continue this pattern.

Step 4: Have the children write the final version on paper and illustrate it.

AL: *The Magic School Bus: Inside the Human Body* correlates with the health and science theme of the month and offers more challenging reading material. Pace the reading and discussion of the book so that it can be completed in three days.

The pictures in this book have a wealth of information that enriches the topic. Encourage the children to bring to class other material that relates to this subject.

After the book has been completed, read it to the whole class and encourage group members to share their knowledge with their classmates.

DAY 3

Why Can't I Fly?

Shared Reading

Step 1: Introduce the story by discussing the author. The children will draw parallels about this story and *More Spaghetti . . .* from the discussion and the cover. Record the predictions about the story for comparison at the conclusion of the session.

Step 2: Read the story together, inviting the children to join in.

Step 3: Ask the students to compare this story to the one read during the first session. In what ways is it different?

Step 4: Record words that are new or difficult for the students. Write these on word cards for use in the small group sessions.

Small Group Instruction

EL: If this group is ready to move on to a new book, do so. If not, continue working with *More Spaghetti, I Say.* The following suggestions are applicable for either book.

- Review the vocabulary, emphasizing decoding skills.

- Find the funniest part in the story and read it out loud. Note words that are especially troublesome.

- Review one or two decoding skills that need to be reinforced for this group.

- Let the children read the book with a partner.

TL:

Step 1: Review vocabulary that may be difficult from this book.

Step 2: Allow the children to choose parts and read the book as a play.

Step 3: Distribute pieces of 12-by-18-inch paper. Have the children fold it into eighths (fold it once, fold it twice, and fold it again). Number the boxes from 1 through 8. Tell the children to sequence the story by writing the name of the character in the appropriate box and then illustrating that part of the story. When this is complete, cut the sections apart and staple them, in order, into a book. Use this to assess sequencing and comprehension skills.

AL: Continue reading *The Magic Schoolbus: Inside the Human Body.*

DAY 4

More Spaghetti, I Say

Shared Reading

Step 1: Ask for some adjectives that describe Minnie and Freddie. Record the responses.

Step 2: Distribute the vocabulary cards made following the previous session.

Step 3: Read the story together. Ask individuals to hold up their words as they appear in the story.

Step 4: Discuss the idea of trying to teach a monkey to fly. Ask if anyone can think of another story that the class has read in which one animal was trying to teach another to fly. (*Bear's Bargain* by Frank Asch) Compare these two stories.

Step 5: Ask which words from either Gellman story rhyme. Record these on a separate paper.

Small Group Instruction

EL:

Step 1: Prepare a cloze activity before the group is called. Write sentences on the board, omitting the vocabulary words.

Step 2: Review the vocabulary words. Place the cards face down on the table. Ask each child to select a card, turn it over, and read it. If they are able to read a word, they can keep it. If they don't know it, they return it to its original location, face down, and the next person has a turn. This variation of "Concentration" is a good way to make vocabulary drill fun.

Step 3: Ask the children to make some sentences using the vocabulary words. Discuss the parts of a sentence. Each has a noun and a verb, is a complete thought (makes sense), begins with a capital letter, and ends with punctuation.

Step 4: Let the children read the book independently or with a friend.

TL:

Step 1: Continue the reinforcement of cause and effect by asking the children to name one of the characters in the book, tell what suggestion it made to help Minnie fly, and specify the result. Record the children's responses.

Step 2: After the children have named all of the ways Minnie tried to fly, ask them to choose one of the characters, turn to that part of the book, and read the section. Allow time for each to have a turn.

119

Step 3: Have the children identify the verbs in the story. Write them on the board.

Step 6: Pass out writing paper. Ask the children to choose five of the verbs and write sentences using these words. Collect the papers upon completion.

Step 7: Review the structure of a sentence, including punctuation and capitalization.

AL: Complete the reading of *The Magic Schoolbus: Inside the Human Body*, and discuss what the children learned. Ask the following questions:

- Is there a part of the body that the bus did not visit about which the children are curious?

- Which part did they find the most interesting? Why?

Provide time for them to look through the pages, make comments, discuss, and ask questions.

DAY 5

Creative Writing

The two books read this week offer inspiration for creative writing.

Step 1: Review with the whole group the ways Minnie tried to fly and how she ate spaghetti. After the discussion, the following titles and activities can suggest ideas to the class for stories (students should, of course, be free to think of others):

How I Tried to Learn to Fly (Swim like a Fish, Climb a Tree like a Squirrel, Hop like a Kangaroo)
My New Recipe for Spaghetti
Why Can't I _____ ? *(student fills in the desired word)*
Write a letter to Minnie, telling her why she can't fly.
Pretend that you are Minnie's mother. You came home from shopping to find spaghetti all over the house. What would you say and do? Would Minnie be punished? If so how?

Step 2: Encourage children to think of other topics. To help with motivation, you might make available some cooked spaghetti for the children to play with while they are thinking.

Independent Activities

Materials

Construction paper

Writing paper

Alphabet pasta

Extension Activities

- Make a rhyme book from the words in the story. Using a literature square or flip-book, write a word on the outside and a rhyming word on the inside. At the bottom of the section, write two sentences with the rhyming words at the end and illustrate them.

  Example: *skate / late.*

  I would love to skate,
  But it would make me late!

- Divide the class into groups of four or five. Have students work together to make a dictionary of favorite foods. They are to print the letter, write the word, and draw a picture of the food. Combine the pages into books.

- Begin a large chart of the different kinds of pasta. Ask the children to bring in one or two pieces of pasta, glue these to the chart, and write the name beneath the pasta. See how many different kinds they can find.

- Research the history of pasta. For information, write to National Pasta Association, 1156 Fifteenth St. N.W., Suite 900, Washington, DC 20005

- The words for the kinds of pasta have other meanings in Italian. Have the children find out what the meanings are. Examples: *macaroni - dearest darling, vermicelli - little worms, mostaccioli - small mustaches.*

- The library has more information about pasta. Make it available to the class during this study so that the children can learn about the topic independently.

Small Group and Center Activities

- Minnie really does want to fly. Invent a way she can fly and, using construction paper, make a model of your invention.

- Pretend that one morning you woke up and there had been an enormous snowstorm. However, instead of snow, pasta fell from the sky. Draw a picture of what you would do outside in the pasta. It can be any kind of pasta.

- Using alphabet pasta, spell a word, glue the pieces of pasta to a piece of paper, and draw a picture of the word.

- Use a garden catalog to find pictures of fruits and vegetables. Cut out the pictures and glue them on cards. Place the cards in a center with two small green plastic boxes (the kind used for strawberries and other small produce). Label the boxes "Fruits" and "Vegetables," and have the children sort the pictures into the appropriate categories.

- Have the children draw and label pictures of their favorite foods. Place these in a center for sorting into similar categories.

Science

Materials

Dry pasta

Plastic glasses

White vinegar

Clear cola

Clear liquid soap

- Pour vinegar, clear cola, and water into different glasses. Don't tell the children what the liquids are. Direct them to drop a piece of pasta into each glass and watch what happens. Record the findings.

- Continue the study of the human body, discussing the following:

The lungs filter oxygen from the air so the blood can carry it to the body.

The brain tells the body what to do; the nervous system is the messenger that delivers the commands.

The skin is a protective covering that keeps germs and foreign objects out of the body. When the body becomes hot, the skin sweats, thus cooling the system.

Math

- How far can children in the class "fly?" Go to the playground and mark a point on the ground. Let each child run to that point and jump. Have a buddy mark the landing point and measure the length of the "flight." Who "flew" the farthest? Whose "flights" were the same length?

- Cut out pictures of various fast foods, or allow the children to draw them. Label each with a price. What combinations can be purchased for one dollar. Have the children write story problems for their combinations and use calculators to check their answers.

Foreign Language

Some form of pasta is found in almost every culture. Teach the children words that would be used if ordering this dish in the language being studied. Which words describe how they want it prepared?

Music

Teach the class "On Top of Spaghetti," and sing it during this week.

Art

Draw pictures to illustrate the action in "On Top of Spaghetti." Go to another class and sing the song, showing the pictures.

Week 4: Overview

Instructional Books

> *Cloudy with a Chance of Meatballs* by Judi Barrett
> *Just Like Abraham Lincoln* by Bernard Waber

Related Titles

> *Wednesday Is Spaghetti Day* by Maryann Cocca-Leffler (to be read aloud)
> *How Pizza Came to Queens* by Dayal Kaur Khalsa (to be read aloud)

Poems

"Oodles of Noodles" by Lucis and James L. Hymes, Jr.
"George Washington" by Winifred C. Marshall
"The Brain" by Jeff Moss
"The Most Interesting Parts of the Body" by Jeff Moss

Objectives

1. **Phonetic skills**
   Review and reinforce vowel diphthongs.
2. **Structural analysis**
   Review possessive pronouns.
   Begin to understand the concept of verb tenses.
3. **Comprehension**
   Review the concept of topic sentences.
   Review and reinforce the concepts of main idea and supporting facts.

Materials

Word cards in the shape of a cloud

Construction paper

Writing paper

Poetry and Skills Session

DAY 1

"Oodles of Noodles"

Step 1: Let a volunteer read the title. Ask what is meant by an "oodle." How much is that? What other words have a similar meaning? Why would the author choose that word?

Step 2: Read the poem together several times.

Step 3: Identify the rhyming words. Change the beginning sound of one of these words to form new words.

DAY 2

"George Washington"

Step 1: Introduce this poem as a motivation for a discussion of Presidents' Day. Encourage the children to name as many presidents as they can. Typically Washington and Lincoln are among the first named.

Step 2: Develop the understanding that these men were once small boys who learned to read and write and enjoyed playing.

Step 3: Ask for ideas about skills that children in the class have that these men did not possess. Examples: They probably could not ride a bike, play computer games, or work a VCR. Discuss reasons that the presidents would not have known about these things. This is a good way to help students understand the differences between their world and that of Washington and Lincoln.

DAY 3

"The Most Interesting Parts of the Body"

Step 1: Begin by asking volunteers to name the parts of the body. They should be somewhat knowledgeable because they have been studying the body this month.

Step 2: Introduce the poem and read it several times. Encourage discussion of the poem.

Step 3: Call attention to the possessive word "someone's," and let a child tell what it means. Expand the concept of possessive words.

Step 4: Read the poem again.

DAY 4

"The Brain"

Step 1: Read this poem without introduction. Read it again, with the children closing their eyes this time.

Step 2: Invite comments about what they were thinking when they listened the second time. Were they seeing "pictures"? If so, what were the pictures?

Step 3: Review and reinforce a phonetic skill that has been difficult for the children.

Step 4: Read the poem again for pleasure.

Step 5: Distribute copies of the poem for your students to illustrate and include in their poetry notebooks.

Reading Instruction

DAY 1

Cloudy with a Chance of Meatballs

Shared Reading

Step 1: Introduce the book in the usual way, asking for predictions and recording them. If a child's initials are written beside his or her prediction, it is appropriate to refer to the child during the summation part by saying, "Joey thought the book would be about the weather. Was that an accurate prediction?" It is important to be sensitive to the feelings of the children when using this technique.

Step 2: Ask the group whether they think the story will take place in a city or a small town. On what do they base their opinions?

Step 3: Introduce the name of the town, "Chewandswallow," and allow the children time to appreciate the humor in the name.

Step 4: Have the group decide which words will be targeted for vocabulary work. Write these words on cards.

Step 5: Read the book with the group.

Small Group Instruction

EL: The book is quite challenging, so have this group rewrite the story, using the targeted vocabulary. Write the story on chart paper as it is dictated, and have the children read it before concluding the session. Make smaller, individual copies for the students before the group meets again.

TL:

Step 1: Review the targeted vocabulary.

Step 2: Read the first part of the book, using directed reading strategies and noting words that pose difficulties for the students.

Step 3: Before the children return to their desks, write some of those words on the board. Use appropriate decoding strategies to help the students read them.

Step 4: Give the children paper. They will fold it, write words in the boxes, illustrate the words, cut the boxes apart, and staple them together. The children can take the finished product home and practice reading the words.

AL:

Step 1: Ask whether anyone in the group knows the definition of a "tall tale"? If no one does, explain that it is a story that is greatly exaggerated.

Step 2: Ask for examples of tall tales. (Paul Bunyan, Pecos Bill)

Step 3: Inquire how the definition of a tall tale relates to *Cloudy with a Chance of Meatballs*. The children should readily understand that this is a tall tale.

Step 4: Send the group to the school library to check out a tall tale, or have copies of other titles available in the classroom. Tell the children to read one of the titles before the next session.

DAY 2

Cloudy with a Chance of Meatballs

Shared Reading

Step 1: Reread the book for pleasure.

Step 2: Invite the children to tell you what makes this a good story. Ask for examples of a story they did not enjoy. What was the difference between the two?

Step 3: Ask whether someone in their family is a good storyteller. Encourage descriptions of people who are talented storytellers. Ask what makes the grandfather in the story a good storyteller.

Step 4: Identify verbs in the story and discuss their use. Point out examples of various tenses.

Small Group Instruction

EL:

Step 1: Have the children read the story they wrote during the previous session.

Step 2: Place the vocabulary cards face up on the table. Have the students find these words in the story, "frame" them, and read the sentence. Help the children place the words in alphabetical order.

Step 3: Tell the children to write another chapter to the story begun in the previous session. If the story is written in such a way that is not appropriate, they can compose a different version.

Step 4: Write it on chart paper as it is dictated, and make individual copies at the conclusion of the group.

Step 5: Distribute the individual copies from the previous session, and ask the students to illustrate them. Collect the copies and put them together in a book at the end of the week.

TL: Read the remainder of the book, using directed reading strategies and focusing on the food that must be cleaned up each day. Brainstorm some unusual ways to perform this job. Record the suggestions.

AL: Have the children share the stories they have read, pointing out the factors that make them tall tales. Let them choose a different title to read for the next session.

DAY 3

Cloudy with a Chance of Meatballs

Shared Reading

Step 1: Reread the first half of the book, stopping at the place where the sanitation department begins its work.

Step 2: Discuss the problems with leftover food. How can they get rid of it? What are some of the disadvantages of having food fall from the sky?

Step 3: Briefly review what constitutes a compound word. Ask the children to name compound words from the story. Write each small word on a card as they name the compound words.

Step 4: Review and discuss verb tenses.

Step 5: Ask the children to choose a paragraph and determine the main idea. Is there a sentence in the paragraph that states this idea? Help them "discover" topic sentences. This skill will not be mastered in one session but will have to be reinforced many times.

Step 6: Ask the class whether they can combine any of the words from the cards (see step 3) to make new compound words.

Small Group Instruction

EL:

Step 1: Review the vocabulary.

Step 2: Write a new chapter or version of the story, record it on chart paper, and make copies for the students.

Step 3: Ask the children to list all of the food that fell from the sky in Chewandswallow. Write their responses on the board. Have them determine categories for the food.

Step 4: Distribute 12-by-18-inch paper. Have the children fold it twice, creating four sections on each side of the sheet. Write the category headings in the sections. The children are to write the name of the food under the appropriate heading.

TL:

Step 1: Begin this session by asking each child to choose two pages in the book to read aloud.

Step 2: Return to the suggestions for cleaning up the leftover food. Ask for new ideas, and add them to the list.

Step 3: Give the children drawing and writing paper. Have them illustrate one of the ideas, write a line or two defining the problem, and then describe the solution. Display the completed work on a bulletin board.

AL:

Step 1: Share the stories at the beginning of the group. As the children tell about the tall tales they have read, write some of the exaggerated events on the board. Analyze these exaggerations.

Step 2: Ask the students how they would go about writing a tall tale. Help them understand that they would take an ordinary event and exaggerate it. Allow time to expand this idea. It may be necessary to give an example to help the children get started: "When I came into the classroom this morning, there were papers all over the floor. The chairs were turned over and books were off the shelves. I couldn't imagine what had made such a mess. Then I looked in the closet. I saw a cricket a yard long, and it was throwing things off the shelves."

Depending upon time and interest, the children may wish to tell how the problem of the huge cricket was solved.

Step 3: Give the children paper on which to write their stories. Inform them that they will read the stories to the group during the next session. Cutting the paper in 18-by-6-inch strips makes a tall paper for a tall tale.

DAY 4

Shared Reading

Step 1: During this session, focus on the feelings of the people in Chewandswallow. At the beginning of the story, they were quite happy in their homes, but conditions changed and it became impossible for them to stay there. How would the students feel about leaving their homes?

Step 2: Compare this part of the story to the Pilgrims' flight.

Step 3: Ask what it would feel like to move to a country where you didn't know anyone, the customs were different, and perhaps you could not speak the language. If there are children in the class who have recently moved, encourage them to share their feelings. Record some of the responses on chart paper. Keep it for the creative writing session on day 5.

Small Group Instruction

EL:

Step 1: Take a few minutes at the beginning of the session to check word recognition. Reinforce decoding skills as needed by individuals in the group.

Step 2: Read the stories written during the previous sessions, and ask the students to frame nouns, verbs, and adjectives.

Step 3: Distribute student copies, which the children will combine in a book. Give them construction paper to make covers, on which they will write a title and the name of author and illustrator.

TL:

Step 1: Have the students read the book individually or with a friend.

Step 2: Ask the children what adjustments the people of Chewandswallow would have to make in their new homes. They have to shop for and prepare their own food. What steps are necessary to accomplish this? Encourage a discussion of what is involved in buying and preparing food.

Step 3: Have the children pretend they are one of the townspeople. Let them write a story about the first time they had to prepare a meal. Describe the problems they might encounter. Add these papers to the display begun the day before.

AL: Have the children read their stories to the group and then identify the exaggerations. If they have not illustrated the stories, give them another "tall" piece of paper for this purpose.

DAY 5

Creative Writing

Step 1: Ask the children to name as many weather terms as they can. Write these on the board.

Step 2: Tell them they may write a tall tale about weather. Give some examples of exaggerations about weather, such as "It was raining cats and dogs," and "The fog was so thick you couldn't see your hand in front of your face."

Step 3: Provide the class with books in a shape that relates to the story. Provide several shapes cut out of a stiff paper or tag board on which the children can trace and cut their own books. They might also draw an original shape on tag board and use it as a pattern for their book.

Step 4: As always, if children have a different idea for a story encourage them to use it. While they are writing, move among the group, offering encouragement and assistance as needed.

Independent Activities

Materials

  Construction paper

  Writing paper

  Brown paper

  Circle patterns for meatballs

  Paper plates

  Pictures of food

Extension Activities

- Let the children work in pairs or small groups to write new weather reports for the town of Chewandswallow. They can pretend to give these reports on television. If they have been bringing weather reports to class on a daily basis, they will be more successful with this activity.

- Tell the students that the mayor of Chewandswallow is up for reelection. Ask what kinds of promises he might make to the people to get their votes.

- Make available some related titles, and have students compare stories. Some suggestions are as follows:

  The Night It Rained Pancakes by Mirra Ginsburg
  Rain Makes Applesauce by Julian Scheer and Marvin Bileck
  The Magic Meatballs by Alan Yaffe

- Write a letter to the author of *Cloudy with a Chance of Meatballs*, Judi Barrett, and ask her questions about the story. Where did she get the idea? How did she invent the name?

- Draw a Venn diagram, and have children compare the town of Chewandswallow with their home town.

Small Group and Center Activities

- Provide brown paper and a pattern for a circle. Have the children cut out "meatballs" and write a word on each one. Combine balls to form compound words, and glue them to a drawing of a bowl.

- Place in a center paper plates and magazines that contain pictures of food. Have the children cut out pictures that show a healthy meal, glue them to the paper plate, and label it "Good for you." Then have them paste pictures of unhealthy food on another plate and label it "Bad for you."

- Ask the children to pretend that they are going to live in the town of Chewandswallow. Have them build a house of construction paper. Ask them to think about the things they need to be safe, happy, and well fed in this strange town.

- Ask the children to invent a raincoat that the people of Chewandswallow would like to wear, draw a picture of it, and tell why it would be good to have one if they lived in this town.

- Have the students think of some other names for Chewandswallow, write them at the bottom of a piece of paper, and draw a picture of the new town.

Science

Materials

White straws

Yarn in different colors

Small balloons, two per child

Wiggly eyes from a craft store, two per child

Pattern for tracing a body

Flesh-colored netting (optional)

Step 1: The study of the body will be completed during this week. Invite a doctor, nurse, or other health care person to speak to the class, answering questions the students may have.

Step 2: Put the pages of the big book together, and make a cover by constructing a body from the following items:

Straws for bones
Red yarn for blood
Small balloons for lungs
Construction paper for heart

Step 3: If desired, glue net over the collage for skin, add small eyes purchased at a craft store, and use yarn for hair. Supply a variety of similar items and let the children "construct" a body.

Step 4: The children should write a final story, using the body on the cover for motivation. The story can be either factual or creative.

Math

- Bring weather forecasts from the newspaper to school. Make a weather graph for the week.

- Record the actual highs each day. Compare them with the weather prediction, and graph the accuracy of the reports.

- Keep individual records of the foods the children eat each day. Tally the healthy items and those that are not so healthy.

- Ask the children to bring in empty food containers (cereal boxes, frozen food boxes, and so on). Show them how to read the ingredients. Discuss the fat, salt, and calorie counts, and determine whether these foods are healthy.

Foreign Language

Summarize the words presented during this unit. The children might enjoy making a picture dictionary of some of the words related to food.

Music

Invite the children to bring in some music that they enjoy. Through the year, they have had many examples of music that correlates with the material presented. Perhaps they deserve some "equal time." It is possible that they will have some suggestions for songs that they think relate to the science unit.

Art

Have the children bring in an assortment of boxes and reproduce the town of Chewandswallow. They can shape newspaper into mountains and paint a backdrop. They can make the townspeople out of stiff paper and stand them in lumps of clay.

Bibliography

Books

Balestrino, Philip. *The Skeleton Inside You*. New York: Scholastic, 1990.

Barrett, Judi. *Cloudy with a Chance of Meatballs*. New York: Aladdin Books, Macmillan, 1978.

Bunting, Eve. *Valentine Bears*. New York: Scholastic, 1993.

Cocca-Leffler, Maryann. *Wednesday Is Spaghetti Day*. New York: Scholastic, 1990.

Cole, Joanna. *The Magic Schoolbus: Inside the Human Body*. New York: Scholastic, 1989.

dePaola, Tomi. *Strega Nona*. New York: Simon and Schuster, 1975.

———. *Big Anthony and the Magic Ring*. Orlando: Harcourt Brace Jovanovich, 1979.

———. *Strega Nona's Magic Lessons*. Orlando: Harcourt Brace Jovanovich, 1982.

Freeberg, Lori. *Learning about Your Body*. Palos Verdes Estates, Calif.: 1988.

Gellman, Rita Golden. *Why Can't I Fly?* New York: Scholastic, 1976.

———. *More Spaghetti, I Say*. New York: Scholastic, 1977.

———. *A Monkey Grows Up*. New York: Scholastic, 1991.

Gross, Ruth. *A Book about Your Skeleton*. New York: Scholastic, 1978.

Hall, Katy. *Skeletons! Skeletons!* New York: Scholastic, 1991.

Hoban, Russell. *Bread and Jam for Frances*. New York: Scholastic, 1964.

Hutchins, Pat. *The Doorbell Rang*. New York: Scholastic, 1987.

Khalsa, Dayal Kaur. *How Pizza Came to Queens*. New York: Clarkson N. Potter, 1989. Reprint, Scholastic, 1989.

Kroll, Steven. *It's Groundhog Day*. New York: Scholastic, 1989.

McClanahan, Susan D. *Breakfast Buffalo*. New York: Macmillan, 1975.

Numeroff, Laura Joffe. *If You Give a Mouse a Cookie*. New York: Harper & Row, 1985.

———. *If You Give a Moose a Muffin*. New York: Scholastic, 1992.

Redhead, Janet Slater. *The Big Block of Chocolate*. Auckland: Ashton Scholastic, 1985.

Schweninger, Ann. *Valentine Friends*. New York: Puffin, Penguin, 1988. Reprint, Scholastic.

Sharmat, Mitchell. *Gregory the Terrible Eater*. New York: Scholastic, 1980.

Slepian, Jan, and Ann Seidler. *The Hungry Thing*. New York: Scholastic, 1967.

———. *The Hungry Thing Returns*. New York: Scholastic, 1990.

Waber, Bernard. *Just Like Abraham Lincoln*. Boston: Houghton Mifflin, 1964.

Poems

Adoff, Arnold. "Chocolate, Chocolate." In *The Random House Book of Poetry for Children,* edited by Jack Prelutsky. New York: Random House, 1983a.

———. "My Mouth." In *The Random House Book of Poetry for Children,* edited by Jack Prelutsky. New York: Random House, 1983b.

Eiland, Kathleen. "If I Were a Valentine" In *Poetry Place Anthology,* edited by Rosemary Alexander. New York: Scholastic, 1983.

Giovanni, Nikki. "The Reason I Like Chocolate." In *The Random House Book of Poetry for Children,* edited by Jack Prelutsky. New York: Random House, 1983.

Hymes, Lucis, and James L. Hymes, Jr. "Oodles of Noodles." In *The Random House Book of Poetry for Children,* edited by Jack Prelutsky. New York: Random House, 1983.

Katz, Bobbie. "Patience." In *The Random House Book of Poetry for Children,* edited by Jack Prelutsky. New York: Random House, 1983.

Marshall, Winifred C. "George Washington." In *Poetry Place Anthology,* edited by Rosemary Alexander. New York: Scholastic, 1983.

Moore, Lilian. "Ground Hog Day." In *The Random House Book of Poetry for Children,* edited by Jack Prelutsky. New York: Random House, 1983.

Moss, Jeff. "The Brain." In *The Butterfly Jar.* New York: Bantam Books, 1989a.

———. "The Most Interesting Parts of the Body." In *The Butterfly Jar.* New York: Bantam Books, 1989b.

Nash, Ogden. "Celery." In *Poetry Place Anthology,* edited by Rosemary Alexander. New York: Scholastic, 1983.

Payne, Nina. "Chocolate Cake." In *The Random House Book of Poetry for Children,* edited by Jack Prelutsky. New York: Random House, 1983.

Prelutsky, Jack. "I'm Hungry." In *The Random House Book of Poetry for Children,* edited by Jack Prelutsky. New York: Random House, 1983.

———. "Jellyfish Stew." In *The New Kid on the Block.* New York: Greenwillow, William Morrow, 1984. Reprint, Scholastic.

Sendak, Maurice. "February." In *Chicken Soup with Rice.* New York: Scholastic, 1987.

Silverstein, Shel. "Spaghetti." In *Where the Sidewalk Ends.* New York: Harper & Row, 1974.

References

Commire, Anne. *Something about the Authors.* Detroit: Gale Research Company, 1971.

Kovacs, Deborah, and James Preller. *Meet the Authors and Illustrators.* New York: Scholastic, 1991.

Norby, Shirley, and Gregory Ryan. *Famous Children's Authors.* Minneapolis: T. S. Denison, 1988.

SCOPE AND SEQUENCE FOR
Learning About Spring with Children's Literature

MARCH

Author: Mercer Mayer

English Skills
- Structural analysis
  - Commas
- Comprehension
  - Drawing conclusions
  - Summarizing
  - Similes
- Parts of a Book

Science Skills
- Dinosaurs
  - Characteristics
  - Earth during dinosaur age
- Our changing Earth

Math Skills
- Measuring
- Weights

APRIL

Author: Leo Leoni

English Skills
- April and May are used to reinforce and reteach phonetic, structural analysis, and comprehension skills

Science Skills
- Mammals
  - Whales
  - Rabbits
- Characteristics of mammals and fish
  - Sharks
- Health
  - Teeth

Math Skills
- Multiplication
- Double digit addition and subtraction

Social Studies Skills
- Map skills

MAY

Author: Robert McClosky

Science Skills
- Deserts
- The Earth's surface

Social Studies Skills
- Maps and globes
- Location of deserts and oceans

SCOPE AND SEQUENCE FOR
Learning About Fall with Children's Literature

SEPTEMBER

Author: Eric Carle

English Skills
- Phonetic Skills
- Vowels
  - Short and long e
    - Short and long o
  - Rhyming Words
  - Structural analysis
    - Nouns
    - Verbs
- Punctuation
  - Capital Letters
  - Periods
  - Comprehension
    - Alphabetical sequence
  - Prediction
    - Word families
    - Sequence of events
    - Number words

Science Skills
- Classifying insects
- Metamorphosis
- Life cycle of insects
- Comparing insects and spiders
- Migration of some insects

Math Skills
- Calendar
- Graphing
- Symmetry
- Counting sets
- Days of the week

OCTOBER

Author: Bill Martin, Jr.

English Skills
- Phonetic Skills
  - Short and long e, u
  - Vowel followed by r
  - ow and ou
- Structural analysis
  - Adjectives
  - Nouns and verbs
  - Root words and endings
  - Compound words
- Comprehension
  - Sequence
  - Cause and effect
  - Main idea
- Punctuation
  - Question marks
  - Capital letters
  - Periods
  - Quotation marks

Science Skills
- Life cycle of a frog
- Seeds
- Plants
- Leaves
- Seasonal changes

Math Skills
- Graphing
- Measuring
- Problem solving
- Story problems

Social Studies
- Christopher Columbus
- Map skills

NOVEMBER

Author: Ludwig Bemelmans

English Skills
  Phonetic Skills
    Vowels
    Short and long a, i
  Word families
  Rule of silent e
  Structural analysis
    Adjectives
    Rhyming words
    Compounds
  Alphabetizing to the first letter
    Comprehension
    Cause and effect
    Prediction

Social Studies Skills
  France
  Map skills
    Purpose
    Use
    Location of cities
  Pilgrims

Math Skills
  Sequencing
  Concept of a dozen

Foreign Language Skills
  Landmarks in Paris
  Comparing common French and
    English terms